THE SPIRIT OF CREATION

John H. Morgan

THE SPIRIT OF CREATION

Using the
Three Biblical Wealth Engines
To Fund Your Calling, Solve Poverty,
and Capitalize the Global Church

John H. Morgan

EQUIP PRESS

Colorado Springs

The Spirit of Creation: Using the Three Biblical Wealth Engines To Fund Your Calling, Solve Poverty, And Capitalize the Global Church. A Theology of Human Flourishing

Copyright © 2025 John H. Morgan

First Edition: 2025
The Spirit of Creation / John H. Morgan
Paperback ISBN: 978-1-958585-98-6
eBook ISBN: 978-1-958585-99-3

Table of Contents

JOHN H. MORGAN

Introduction
The Spirit of Creation

FLIES SURROUNDED THE CRIPPLED BOY'S face and went in and out of the side of his mouth. He didn't seem to notice, but I couldn't stop watching. I was of a similar age. I was with my parents in Juarez, Mexico, in the 1960s as they guided visiting friends through that town's markets and glass-blowing factories. We lived across the border in El Paso, Texas and frequently traveled to Juarez and cities deeper into Mexico.

Juarez, in those days, was an underdeveloped city. The backstreets were dirt roads, and poverty was everywhere. On this day, it was the middle of summer, and the poor crippled boy sat on a filthy hot street corner begging for himself and his family.

I couldn't quit thinking about that boy, and I felt guilt and relief as we got back in our air-conditioned car and drove back across the border to the U.S. I couldn't imagine being crippled and placed out on a dirty street corner to beg in the blazing heat. Why was I so lucky to be able to walk and live a life of luxury?

That scene and many others like it in poverty spaces burned into my mind questions that I had to answer for myself and for the benefit of anyone I could help. I had to learn what caused poverty, what caused people and communities to flourish, and what we could do to help create the latter. My father was a pastor, and I traveled with him on mission trips to poverty spaces worldwide. Later I served as a pastor and led mission trips to poverty spaces. Each one deepened my sense of calling to understand the causes of poverty and to apply the cures.

I have no idea why God chooses or allows some to be born in the worst of human conditions and others to be born into good conditions. We call it God's sovereignty, but why he chooses or allows some to suffer so much is a mystery that only God can answer.

However, there are biblically rooted, economically sound, and historically proven answers to the questions of what causes poverty and what causes human prosperity. We can learn from them for our benefit and to help those who want to rise from *want* to *enough* and, in some cases, to *abundance*. We can also learn from them to fund the great causes we love, including the Christian mission.

The Spirit of Creation is a biblical worldview for human flourishing. It is the ethos of the three biblical wealth engines, along with the ten requisite policies and infrastructures, that enable them.

This Spirit of Creation can fund your life and calling, solve poverty, and capitalize the Global Church to change the world.

This is a practical theology of economics that can change lives, communities, and nations.

This may sound overwhelming, but it is not. It is understandable, logical, and practical.

The thesis of this book is that the causes of poverty and the cures that create human prosperity can be understood in a metaphor that we call the Tree of Life. It looks like this:

THE TREE OF LIFE THAT SOLVES POVERTY AND CREATES HUMAN FLOURISHING

4. The **fruit** is the spiritual, social, and material wealth created by the people.

3. The **branches** are the 10 infrastructures that support the Spirit of Creation.

2. The **trunk** is the 10 policies that support the Spirit of Creation.

1. The **roots** are the critical mass of people who possess the Spirit of Creation.

The Tree of Life

When conditions 1-3 exist in a community or nation, the automatic result is 4. People create spiritual, social, and material value. They create wealth of every kind.

John H. Morgan

This book will explain points 1-3 and how they can be implemented. It will explain how #1 is the root cause and how establishing it should be the first step in solving poverty and creating prosperity. Most efforts to solve poverty focus on #3, infrastructure. Few efforts are focused on #2, policies. All three are required. When they exist, the people create the fruit of human prosperity and flourishing.

The principles of this book work for everyone. However, my first concern is the global Christian community because they are the Body of Christ, and Jesus Christ is the hope of the world. I want them to flourish in their lives and ministries because they are called to bless the world. They are called to save souls, solve poverty, and redeem culture. So, just like a person in an airplane is instructed to put their oxygen mask on first before they help someone else with their mask, my first concern is the Christian community.

To my Christian brothers and sisters: this practical theology of economics will empower you to fund your life, solve poverty, and capitalize the Global Church. It will empower you to help create human flourishing in every way.

I have seen it work. I have seen many impoverished people gain this Spirit of Creation and change their destinies. Their children will not be placed on a hot, dirty street corner to beg for themselves and their families. They will grow up in families with the spirit to create value in multiple ways that make their livings, help others, and honor God.

I have also seen it work in the U.S. I have seen many people build wealth engines that fund their lives, their callings, and life-changing ministries. I have seen some who practice the principles of this book make and give millions to great causes and ministries.

My goal is not to make you rich, although some will become rich. I aim to teach you the timeless truths to fund your life and calling, solve poverty, and capitalize the Global Church. If we do that, it will change not only our lives and our nation, it will change the world. The Church will thrive. Evangelism, discipleship, and church planting will explode. More and more poverty will be solved in Jesus' name. Cultures will be transformed and redeemed. And people of all beliefs and non-beliefs will be blessed.

That's all I want: to change your life and to change the world.

To understand the Spirit of Creation, we first need to establish some foundational truths about Christ's Kingdom, his truth, and his calling. That is where we will start in the following three chapters.

Chapter One
His Kingdom

IT STARTED WITH A FEVER. Then, the two-year-old girl began to cough. Soon came vomiting and diarrhea. American parents might diagnose it as the flu or some other virus. But to a mother in a small Kenyan village, the symptoms were all unmistakable signs of the unthinkable: malaria.

Her husband, a busy local pastor, was away ministering in some other villages, so she had to deal with the emergency on her own. She walked several kilometers to another village on a quest for medicine. But the clinic turned her away because she didn't have $3.00 worth of Kenyan shillings to pay for it. So she trekked back to her village to find the money.

All the while, the little girl kept getting sicker.

The distraught mother managed to scrape together funds from friends and family and walked back to the other village to purchase the medicine. Then, another long walk home. By the time she got there, her daughter was dead.

This happened just as I began my work in Africa. To this day, I still feel ill from sharing that story. But it's an accurate snapshot of what life is like in too much of the world. There were an estimated 619,000 malaria deaths worldwide in 2021. Approximately three out of four people who die from malaria are children. It kills about half a million children per year. And 94% of all these casualties were in Africa.[1] Malaria is an infectious disease caused by a parasite and transmitted via mosquitos. But what makes it so deadly is something else, something even more lethal. Poverty.

You may not care about the poverty of others, but you probably do care about having enough that you and your family can live with dignity. You might even care about having enough to fund your sense of God's calling on your life, whether in religion, business, nonprofit work, education, science, government service, art, or entertainment.

My message is this: the Spirit of Creation is the biblical path to creating the material resources you need for your life and calling, no matter your socio-economic situation. It also solves poverty and creates productivity and prosperity. It is the biblical pathway to human flourishing.

To understand the Spirit of Creation, we must start with biblical theology. Specifically, we need to understand the theology of God's kingdom, his truth, and his calling.

KINGDOM THEOLOGY FIRST

The Spirit of Creation is built on the three biblical wealth engines. These wealth engines are God's method for us to create some critical parts of his kingdom on earth.

The Bible teaches that the Lord Jesus Christ is the organizing principle of all things (Colossians 1:15-17).

Jesus taught that the kingdom of God is the objective of his work. God created us to know him, love him, and serve his kingdom.

JESUS' CORE MESSAGE WAS THE KINGDOM OF GOD

Jesus' core message was the kingdom of God. That may seem strange because fundamentalism and evangelicalism's core message is the gospel of salvation through faith in Jesus Christ. Jesus called people to faith in him for salvation, especially in one-on-one and small group conversations. However, he did not preach a modern evangelical-style gospel sermon to a crowd. He preached about the kingdom of God. His point was that God is the ultimate reality, and his kingdom is the expression of that reality for which we were created. The obvious application is that we better do what it takes to be members of God's kingdom. The gospel, or good news, is that we can become members of God's family and kingdom through faith in Jesus Christ.

The difference may seem trivial, but it is not. The gospel by itself tends to be man-centered, but the kingdom of God is God-centered. The gospel is about what God did for us and how we can receive it. The kingdom of God is about God and his purposes, and it is a warning that we had better be part of that eternal kingdom, or we will be doomed to eternal punishment with Satan and all others who reject it. The kingdom's focus is clear: everything is first and foremost about God, not us. And we are blessed to be in a relationship with God and to participate in his kingdom. It is our highest purpose and privilege.

I think the focus on ourselves has been the reason for the spiritual decline of the American church in my generation. It has become one more consumer choice for a happy life rather than an absolute imperative.

In contrast, the book of Romans, which is the theology of salvation, starts with the problem of the wrath of God against sinful people who have violated and vandalized everything about his character and creation. They are usurpers of his kingdom. Then, the solution of salvation through faith in Jesus Christ is explained. The great historical sermon, *Sinners in the Hands of an Angry God*, by Jonathan Edwards in 1741 was the catalyst for the First Great Awakening. It is not typical of the sermons preached today. It exposed people's guilt for their sinful violations of God's character and kingdom before it offered the solution of salvation.

Jesus' first, lengthiest, and most important message was the Sermon on the Mount, in Matthew 5-7. Parts of it are also found in the Gospels of Mark and Luke. Snippets and concepts from it are found in the Gospel of John.

The subject of the Sermon on the Mount was the kingdom of God. The predicate was how people who are citizens of this kingdom behave righteously. Jesus gave multiple examples of this, from people's life attitudes to their religious practices to their relationships with all kinds of people. It exposed people's hearts and true relationship with God.

The second most important sermon by Jesus was his last before his death, the Olivet Discourse, in Matthew 24-25. It was his response to the disciples' question, "What will be the sign of your coming and of the end of the age?" (Matthew 24:3b). It was Jesus' most important statement on prophecy and his Second Coming. In it, he said, "At that time the kingdom of heaven will be like… (Matthew 25:1)," and after he comes and judges people, he said, "Then the King will say to those on his right; take your inheritance, the kingdom prepared for you since the creation of the world," (Matthew 25:34). The subject is the kingdom of God and the predicate is that it will come in its fullness at Jesus' Second Coming when the things he said are fulfilled.

Between Jesus' first and last sermons, the kingdom of God was his core message.

Acts 1:3b says, "He [Jesus] appeared to them over a period of forty days and spoke about the kingdom of God. The final two verses of Acts say, "For two whole years Paul stayed there [Rome] in his own rented house and welcomed all who came to see him. Boldly and without hindrance, he preached the kingdom of God and taught about the Lord Jesus Christ" (Acts 28:30-31). Jesus taught his kingdom theology to the apostles, who also taught it.

JESUS DEFINED THE KINGDOM OF GOD AS GOD'S WILL BEING DONE

Jesus defined the kingdom of God as God's will being done. When Jesus was teaching us how to pray in Matthew 6:10 in the Sermon on the Mount, he said to pray, "Thy kingdom come thy will be done on earth as it is in heaven." The two first phrases are not different ideas; they are the same idea, which was said twice in different ways. They are parallel statements. "Thy kingdom come," and "thy will be done," are the same. Jesus was saying God's kingdom exists anywhere and to the extent that God's will is done.

God's will is done completely in heaven, where his subjects are completely obedient. On earth, it is a mixed outcome because we have free will, and we are living under the influence of the fall of humanity into sin and the ongoing influence of Satan and his kingdom of darkness. Christians also live under the influence of God's Spirit, his Word, and his kingdom. Different people do (or don't) obey God to different degrees. Jesus was saying to pray for more people to obey God more on earth, as citizens of his kingdom, which will bring a measure of his kingdom to earth as they do. To the degree that they obey God in their family relationships, the kingdom of God will exist there. To the degree that they treat others as God would have them, his kingdom exists there. To the degree that their religious practices obey God's will, his kingdom is there. To the degree that their work and economic practices obey God, his kingdom exists there.

JESUS' KINGDOM TEACHING BRINGS US BACK TO OUR ORIGINAL PURPOSE

The Old Testament makes it clear that as Creator, God is the king of all. Psalm 2 teaches that God is the King of everything, that earthly kings who oppose him will perish, and that he will give his son the ultimate Kingship over everything. The conclusion is, "Kiss his son, or he will be angry, and your way will lead to destruction, for his wrath can flare up in a moment. Blessed are all who take refuge in him." (Psalm 2:12)

Our original purpose given in Genesis 1:28 was to, "Be fruitful, multiply, fill the earth, subdue it, and take dominion [of it]." We will unpack this verse in Chapter Four in more detail, but for now, the summary of this verse is this: our original purpose was to create new and better things on earth to make our livings, to bless others, to make the world a better place, and to serve God.

As the Bible's revelation progressed over time, all of God's domain was called his kingdom. In light of the whole Bible, we can now see that the original purpose was to do these things to represent, serve, and grow God's kingdom on earth.

WE HAVE A KINGDOM CULTURE CALLING

We have a kingdom culture calling. Our first purpose, before sin entered the world, was to make great human culture on earth as emissaries and expanders of God's kingdom. But sin entered the world and corrupted much of it. So, Christ came to redeem us and eventually all things. Our job now is the Cultural Commission of making the world a better place *and* the Great Commission of making disciples, found in Matthew 28:18-20.

This is the message of Charles Colson's book, *How Now Shall We Live.*

It is our contention in this book that the Lord's cultural commission is inseparable from the great commission. That may be a jarring statement for many conservative Christians, who, through much of the twentieth century, have shunned the notion of reforming culture, associating the concept with the liberal social gospel. The only task of the church, many

> *fundamentalists and evangelicals have believed, is to save as many lost souls as possible from a world literally going to hell. But this implicit denial of a Christian worldview is unbiblical, and it is the reason we have lost so much of our influence in the world. Salvation does not consist simply of freedom from sin; salvation also means being restored to the task we were given in the beginning – the job of creating culture.*[2]

To summarize, our original human purpose was to create a good culture in obedience to God. Now, our redeemed Christian purpose is to restore a good culture that reflects the will of God and his kingdom. We must save souls and create good culture to grow Christ's kingdom. Both of these require material resources, and God gives us the way to create them.

THE SPIRIT OF CREATION FUNDS OUR KINGDOM WORK

I believe that the ministries that are spiritually *and* economically empowered have the greatest impact. Few people will say so because it doesn't sound as spiritual as saying that spiritual empowerment solves everything. But God created the spiritual and the material parts of his kingdom; they are ruled by his principles that govern each of them, and we must have the resources of both to do his will.

The Spirit of Creation and the Three Biblical Wealth Engines create biblical economic empowerment. They create the knowledge and skills to generate the resources people need for their lives and callings.

In American Christian culture, we take a lot of this for granted because so much of it was built into the assumptions and principles of our country's founding. It is natural for many of us to act on the Three Biblical Wealth Engines and not realize that they are biblical and a big part of the success of our ministries.

Let me illustrate the power of spiritual and economic empowerment from an example from the Majority World. The Majority World is Africa, Asia, Latin America, and Oceania. It's where most people live and where two-thirds of the Global Church lives. Allow me to tell you about my friend George, who lives in Kenya, Africa.

GEORGE'S STORY

I couldn't believe it when we drove up to this school in rural western Kenya. 380 kids dressed in blue uniforms were gathered on the sloping quad in the middle of the school's block and tin classrooms and dormitories. The boys wore their blue Bermuda shorts with white shirts and grey V-neck sweaters. The girls wore their blue plaid skirts with white shirts and grey V-neck sweaters. They all wore black shoes with white socks. And they were excited.

They gathered and sang songs for us. My hosts asked me to bring a gospel message to them, which I did. I challenged them to receive Christ and his purpose for their lives, and many responded with prayers of faith. That was my introduction to Golden State Academy in Migori County, Kenya, outside of the town of Awendo, in 2020.

Ten years earlier, I led a training event on the Three Wealth Engines in Nairobi for a group of Christian leaders who worked in ministry, business, education, and government. George Kienga was there. He was quiet, but he was taking the teaching to heart. He traveled from Migori County to Nairobi for this training because he could not support his family with his job as a math teacher and his small plot farm. He was hungry physically, spiritually, emotionally, and intellectually. He needed a better way to live out his calling in Christ's kingdom.

He went home and began to apply what he had learned. He went to his farming neighbors and told them that for a small tuition, he would receive their preschool kids at his house, he would feed them some porridge, and he would teach them their preschool lessons. The next year he added kindergarten. Then he added first grade, and so on. He kept hiring teachers and growing his school. He sat down with the farmers and taught them what he had learned about the Three Wealth Engines so they could increase their production to pay their children's tuition to his school. And Golden State Academy has thrived.

When I visited George and his academy, I saw three tractors with big sugar cane trailers hitched to them. "Whose are those?" I asked him. He grinned with a tooth missing and said, "They're mine. We use them to contract sugar cane harvesting in our county." He had been expanding his farming operations and acquired these tractors in that process.

Then he took me to the new home he had built in the previous few years. It was very nice. We had a lovely lunch there with his wife and children, and he pointed out several plots of land in the area that he had added to his farming business. His seventy-year-old father drove up on an enduro motorcycle and hopped off for lunch with us. George had hired him to supervise his farms. It was a picture of a blessed family.

I visited again in 2022. George's latest venture was building a community medical clinic. The shell of the building was completed, and they were working to finish the interior. The academy had grown to 420 students with grades pre-K through 8th and was ranked first in academic scores for their county. They were adding on to the school facilities. He had also bought several more farms and upgraded some of his harvesting equipment.

Next, George has a vision to build a teaching hospital with a medical school to serve his region, which is underserved in medical services. He is probably going to seek venture capital for this project. He owns the land, he can get the required permits and licenses, and he is working on his business plan to seek funding.

Also, every year in August, George hosts his Biblical Economic Empowerment Youth Conference. A youth in that context means anyone under thirty-five years of age. He is growing a whole community of entrepreneurs who have come out of those conferences.

When I am with George, I can tell he is the king of his county in respect and admiration. He is a spiritual, educational, business, and social leader. He teaches others in his county the Spirit of Creation. He incorporates it into his school curriculum so those students will understand how to fund their lives and callings. His school subsidizes 100 children as boarding students from backgrounds of extreme poverty, most of whom are orphans. He is an elder and leader in his church. He is an evangelist, a disciple maker, a community developer, and a kingdom of God builder. He is living out the whole gospel to the whole person and his whole community.

Here is the kicker: it was all funded by George and his Kenyan neighbors by using the Three Biblical Wealth Engines. If you have ever worked in the developing world, you know how astounding that is. Thousands of well-funded schools, orphanages, missions, and ministries are doing great work in Kenya, like in many other developing countries, but they are almost all supported by outside money from the West. The concept that national Christians can learn to solve their own poverty and fund their own callings doesn't seem to even be on the radar for the vast majority of Christians who work in the poverty space. There seems to be a subtle prejudice that they are incapable of it and that the principles apply only to Western Christians. There is a subtle message of discrimination that the local and national Christians can't do because they are incapable. But this is not true because all people are created in the image of God. All Christians have the Spirit of God and the principles of God's word work for everyone with enough freedom to apply them.

I could have started this book with stories of Americans who have used the Three Biblical Wealth Engines, and I will tell some American stories before this book is finished, but I wanted to make the point that these principles and practices work everywhere. I also wanted to share a story from Kenya that was the opposite of the little girl who died because of her family's lack of $3 to buy her malaria medicine.

George, like many other Christians, had a calling and was spiritually empowered, but he lacked true economic empowerment to accompany his spiritual empowerment. He needed a way to fund his life, family, and calling. He is an example of what has been proven thousands of times. Those who are economically and spiritually empowered in their callings have the greatest impact.

You, too, have a life, and probably a family, and a calling that needs to be properly funded. You are trying to grow the kingdom of God. You need to fund these things, and God's plan is for you to do that through the Spirit of Creation and the Three Biblical Wealth Engines.

We will be teaching you these things, but first, we need to lay some more of the foundation with two more points of biblical theology: God's truth and his calling. In the next chapter, we will look at God's truth. How we view it will make a key difference in understanding these things.

Chapter Two
His Truth

THE SPIRIT OF CREATION IS based on a broad appreciation of God's truth that is missing from much of Christianity today. It is time we recovered it.

WHY HAS NO ONE EVER TOLD US THIS?

My Kenyan friend Shem Okello asked, "Why hasn't anyone ever told us this before?"

His question was laced with a surprising amount of anger because he was normally a good-natured guy.

He asked this in 2010 after I taught him and that group of Kenyan Christian leaders in Nairobi the Three Biblical Wealth Engines. We get the same question almost everywhere in the Majority World where we introduce these truths.

What he was saying was, why didn't the Western Christian missionaries, during his lifetime or his father's, teach them the biblical principles that solve poverty and create enough for them to flourish, fund their lives, and fund their ministries? Why would the Western missionaries leave them unempowered, poor, and dependent on Western charity and aid?

What compounded his frustration was that the Southern Baptist International Missions Board had recently declared Kenya a reached nation. That meant they were pulling their missionaries and funds out of Kenya and sending them elsewhere. Shem and his ministry partners were dependent upon them and their funds. It felt like abandonment without empowerment. It felt like a cruel joke.

At that time, Shem had been the secretary general of the Kenya Baptists for seventeen years. He had been well-trained in the Evangelical view of the Bible and ministry, but his people were stuck in poverty. After he saw the biblical pathway for the first time, he believed it, and he was inspired by it, but he was angry about how long it took to hear about it from Christians who had benefitted from it themselves.

"I don't know why," I answered. "I don't think Christian missionaries understood these things because they were never taught. But I am here teaching you now." I felt a bit defensive toward the well-intentioned and sincere missionaries, and I have known many who did their best with what they knew and what their system taught them. I felt defensive for the Southern Baptists and the International Missions Board, which has done (and is doing) great work worldwide. Still, something is missing in the modern missions movement and methods.

It has missed a kingdom culture theology because evangelicalism and fundamentalism have missed a broader appreciation of God's truth. This has led to a lack of a biblical worldview for solving poverty and creating human flourishing. This has led to three kinds of tunnel vision.

EVANGELICAL TUNNEL VISION

Evangelical tunnel vision is a hyper-focus on our purpose of evangelism to the neglect of our kingdom culture mission. It results in our irrelevance to the culture, a misrepresentation of God to the world, and a ridiculous reductionism, at times, of our gospel message. It becomes a partial gospel instead of the whole gospel to the whole person for the whole world.

When we miss our kingdom culture mission with a tunnel vision on evangelism, we become irrelevant to the pressing problems of our world because only one thing is relevant to us. In his profound *Letter from the Birmingham Jail*, Dr. Martin Luther King, Jr. made a case for the civil rights movement in response to criticism from local clergymen. He said, "I have heard so many ministers say, 'Those are social issues which the gospel has nothing to do with,' and I have watched so many churches commit themselves to a completely otherworldly religion which made a strange distinction between bodies and souls, the sacred and the secular."[3]

In the case of the civil rights movement, the evangelical church was largely absent and irrelevant. We missed the truth that the gospel is social because it touches and redeems every part of human culture. In the case of biblical economics for human flourishing, again, we have been absent. I have been with Shem in villages filled with hungry orphans in a Christian country that has had the gospel for more than 100 years. Yet, a biblical economic understanding and ethic have not become the culture of Kenyan Christianity. There are many evangelistic rallies, and we don't deny their importance. However, what has been neglected is lifting people out of deadly poverty and the degrading bondage of charity and aid.

This tunnel vision is also a misrepresentation of God. It communicates that he is limited in his domain and interests, when in fact, "The earth is the Lord's and everything in it, its people and all who dwell in it" (Psalm 24:1). A fuller and deeper understanding of all of God's word and truth will lead us to appreciate this and represent it to others.

Finally, evangelical tunnel vision leads us at times to a ridiculous reductionism of our gospel message. First, we reduce our purpose to solely evangelism because it is the most important thing, which is a logical fallacy. Just because one thing is the most important, it doesn't mean other things and their totality are not important and necessary. Just because we might say our faith or our families come first does not mean we should quit our jobs to focus on them and neglect to create the income we need for our families. Life is more complex than simplistic reductions. There are multiple important things that we must do and keep in balance.

Then, we reduce the gospel message itself to absurdity. We present a trite sinners' prayer and tell people they got saved if they said it. In truth, genuine faith requires a change of mind, heart, and will toward God. A person might have genuine faith when they say a sinner's prayer, or they very well may not. But too often evangelicals have presented the proper response to the gospel as if it were a repeat-after-me exercise rather than serious business of souls with God.

NEW TESTAMENT TUNNEL VISION

Evangelical tunnel vision leads to (and sometimes flows from) a New Testament tunnel vision. This is the view that the Old Testament is less important because the real message of the gospel and the real handbook of the Church is in the New Testament. Some even neglect the Gospels in the New Testament because they predate the birth of the Church.

Instead, we need to understand that the Old Testament and the Gospels are a vital part of God's word that we must understand and be nourished by. In Romans 11, the Apostle Paul taught that the Church and specifically the Gentiles in the Church have been grafted into the olive tree of Israel. This is his metaphor to explain the relationship of Old Testament Israel to the New Testament Church. The practice of grafting is when an arborist cuts a sapling fruit tree in the middle of its trunk and then re-attaches the top of it to the bottom half of another slightly different kind of tree. The result is a tree that gives better fruit. I have two peach trees in my yard that I bought from a local nursery. They had both been grafted as saplings. It's common practice in fruit tree husbandry. Paul said the same principle applies to the Gentile Church and Israel.

> *If some of the branches have been broken off, and you, though a wild olive shoot, have been grafted in among the others and now share in the nourishing sap from the olive root, do not boast over those branches. If you do, consider this: you do not support the root, but the root supports you. (Romans 11:17-18)*

When we focus on the New Testament and neglect the Old Testament, we are, in a way, boasting and saying our Testament supports the Old Testament and what God did through Israel in ages past. But the truth is that the nourishing sap from the Old Testament gives us the support, framework, and context for the New Testament and life itself.

In addition, Jesus Christ, who is the eternal *logos* of God (John 1:1-2), is the author of the whole Bible. It is incorrect to only ascribe the letters in red that some versions of the New Testament use for the words of Jesus in the Gospels as being the only words of Jesus. Jesus, God's eternal Word, is the divine author of all of it. He is the divine author of Genesis through Revelation. We need to have a more accurate Christology and Bibliology.

This is especially important when we talk about a biblical theology of economics. The Three Wealth Engines come from the first five books of the Bible, especially the book of Genesis. God gave us so much foundational truth about life in the Old Testament, and we can only appreciate it if we value it and study it.

BIBLE TUNNEL VISION

Bible tunnel vision is the hyper-focus on the Bible to the neglect of the truths God reveals through his created world. God gives us certain truths through the special revelation of his Word. He gives us other truths through the general revelation found in his creation. Some sources of truth from general revelation are the observations of how creation works and experimentation to test our ideas of what might work: this is the scientific method and reason.

The Bible teaches us how to gain eternal life, how to live ethically in this life, and other principles of wisdom for living well. It is not a technical manual for every detail of life and work. That's not its purpose. For that, God gave us the stable laws of the universe and our *imago* intelligence from being created in the *Imago Dei* – the image of God. Throughout history, human knowledge about many subjects has grown as new truths are discovered and developed.

The Three Wealth Engines are part of a body of knowledge called Economics. Specifically, it is part of a category of Economics called *normative economics*. That is, which economic principles and practices create human flourishing, and what beliefs and behaviors lead to poverty and human degradation?

The Three Wealth Engines are historically proven, economically sound, and biblically grounded. When we look back at human communities historically, we see that those who practiced the Three Wealth Engines prospered, and those who didn't did not. That's still the case today. The school of economics we consider the most sound or logically consistent and historically accurate is the Austrian School of Economics. Some of its more famous proponents have been Ludwig Von Mises, F.A. Hayek, and Henry Hazlitt. Milton Friedman, Thomas Sowell, and George Gilder are some of its more modern proponents. After years of studying biblical theology and economics as separate disciplines, I had an epiphany. *The three most important principles I saw for human flourishing from my economics study are also taught in the Bible.* In fact, they are taught in the first book of the Bible, and the first and most important principle is taught in the first chapter of the Bible. That's why I call them the Three *Biblical* Wealth Engines.

That realization changed my life. Suddenly, the principles of human flourishing were not only good information from secular sources but also carried the authority of God's Word. These truths are a key part of my calling as a leader in our Kingdom Culture Mission.

That could have only come to me because I had spent years reading in the secular field of economics and history and studying formally in the secular field of organizational leadership. I had gained knowledge from the Word and the world of God, and I could integrate the two. This view and pursuit of truth are necessary to understand things like the causes of and cures for poverty.

WHEATON, WE HAVE A PROBLEM

Many Christians were blindsided by the tyrannical shutdowns imposed by the government during the Covid-19 debacle in 2022, and they spiritualized their response with so-called higher clichés, like "God is in control" and "We must not offend those who are scared" and "Wearing masks is a form of love." Meanwhile, they participated in America's largest experiment in state control of everyone, especially churches, without any sense of danger.

Another area of concern is that our national culture is being hijacked with a new national religion of gender confusion and sexual perversion.

Within the Christian mission, our missions enterprises have largely passed the churches in developing countries off to national leaders in places like Kenya and the Philippines without teaching them the principles and practices to fund their lives and ministries to maximize their part in moving the Christian movement forward.

One of the banes of Western Christianity and the Majority Church is the fallacy of the Prosperity Gospel. It preaches that Christians are entitled to wealth, and the way to activate it is through religious hocus-pocus. It creates a corrupt class of clergy whose theology forces them to live in materialism to prove their bone fides in the religion they preach, and it frustrates their people with nonsense. It is false teaching, plus it doesn't work.

All of these errors flow from not understanding some of God's truths that come from studying God's world and lead me to say metaphorically,

"Wheaton, we have a problem," since Wheaton is one of the epicenters of Christianity in the U.S. I could also say, "Dallas or Atlanta or just about anywhere," but we have a problem.

The problem seems to be that we are so spiritually minded in our view of truth that we have become no earthly good in the practical things of life. We can quote the Bible forward and backward, but we can't integrate it with other key areas of truth to develop solutions to big real-world problems. To start with, Christians, like most people, don't read. And they especially don't read serious subjects other than the Bible and Christian literature. They don't read history, philosophy, political theory, economics, or important biographies. The trend among young pastors that I see is to avoid formal education of any kind and to become slick communicators with as big of a platform as they can create. Besides, all they need to understand is evangelism and some basic discipleship, and they have mastered the Christian message, so they think. They are in the content business (like so many other influencers and entrepreneurs), but their content is weak. They love the saying, "God does not call the qualified; he qualifies the called." They are a mile wide in technique and technology and an inch deep in truth. They are blinded, like a lot of the rest of Christianity, by the tunnel visions of Evangelicalism, the New Testament, and the Bible.

BACK TO SHEM, MY CAPITALIZED KENYAN FRIEND

My friend Shem Okello overcame his anger at not being taught the biblical principles of economic empowerment by the missionaries earlier in his life, and he began to implement the Three Biblical Wealth Engines.

Within a year, he purchased land to build a house, and he hired a contractor to build it.

"I never knew it was better to own one's house than to rent it," Shem told me when he attended that first training, "I have been renting my house for a long time."

"I will have it paid off in five years," he told me after he moved into his new home.

"I wish I could pay mine off in five years," I replied.

Then he became a serial entrepreneur, creating multiple businesses: a tourist transportation business, a tourist guest house, a three-story twelve-unit apartment building, a chicken hatchery, a hair salon, a meat market, a medical clinic with apartment rentals for three doctors on the property, and multiple other rental properties.

One of his rental properties has a group of simple traditional mud huts with thatched roofs that he had built on vacant land near a university in Nairobi. He thought some university students who needed low-cost housing and had moved in from the villages could be his tenants. He expected to rent his huts for 750 Kenyan shillings per month. One day, he met a group of students who wanted to see the huts.

"How much is the rent?" they asked.

"How much would you be willing to pay?" he replied.

They asked to confer with each other under an acacia tree on the edge of the property.

They came back and said, "1,500 Kenyan shillings a month."

"Deal!" Shem said.

Shem was on fire.

In 2022, after seeing the inadequate healthcare options in Kenya during the Covid-19 pandemic, Shem gathered Dr. Shem Okumu and a group of Kenyan professionals, and they started the for-profit Emmanuel Community Hospital in the underserved neighborhood of Chakaa in Nairobi. Their vision is to deliver quality healthcare, spiritual care, and economic growth.

The funny part is that Shem wanted to be a doctor when he was a boy, but he did not have the grades to get accepted to the schools that would lead to medical school. His father, a schoolmaster, was very upset with him about that. Shem carried the pain of that disappointment for a long time. However, Shem became a medical entrepreneur, employer, and leader of doctors.

Shem also maintained a busy schedule of leading multiple ministries of evangelism, discipleship, church planting, caring for widows and orphans, and teaching People Prosper International's Biblical Economic Empowerment training in Kenya, Uganda, and Tanzania. He was an icon of Kenyan economic empowerment, cultural engagement, and Christian ministry leadership. He was a leader of the First Commission and the

Great Commission, and they fully complemented one another. He was a Kingdom culture leader.

Understanding God's kingdom causes us to appreciate the work of putting The Spirit of Creation and the Three Wealth Engines to work for human flourishing.

Understanding the fullness of God's truth in his Word and world causes us to understand the truth and the urgency of the Three Biblical Wealth Engines.

One more piece of foundational truth is needed to appreciate the Spirit of Creation. That is the truth of God's calling. God's calling on your life needs to be resourced, and his method for resourcing it is the Spirit of Creation. Understanding this puts first things first. Calling precedes and supersedes money in importance. Money is a tool, a resource, to enable calling. So, we must prioritize our calling first to avoid the pitfalls of materialism and keep the virtues of our Kingdom Culture Mission.

And calling is the topic of the next chapter.

Chapter Three
His Calling

I KNOCKED ON THE DOOR to meet one of the staff members of the church in New Mexico where I was interviewing to become the Lead Pastor. He was working on his computer and jumped down from his chair and came over to meet me. I was a bit shocked. No one told me a really short guy named Tim Hargrove was on the church staff.

We greeted each other, and I wondered what his story was.

He became one of my best colleagues and partners in both pastoral ministry and the work of our nonprofit, People Prosper International (PPI). Tim is four foot eight inches tall and is called to and gifted at teaching, coaching, leadership, and developing leaders. People notice him when he walks into a room because of his height and engaging personality. He is the guy who is talking to people and laughing with them. When he has been working with a community of people for some time, they deeply love him because of the way he invests in their personal growth.

He did that at the church he and I pastored in New Mexico for many years and for some time when he planted a church in Vancouver, British Columbia. He does that now in some corporate and workforce training programs and for our nonprofit. He is our Global Program Director and is developing leaders for our organization in the Philippines, Cambodia, Thailand, Africa, and beyond.

But Tim had a tough start. He was born with a bone disease that caused his bones in childhood to be extremely brittle. He had broken 43 bones by the time he was thirteen years old. His femur broke twice while his mother was just holding him as an infant. All the bone breaks in his legs caused him to lose normal height.

He lived in a wheelchair for most of his childhood and through high school. His mother broke the barriers for the school district where he lived in Roswell, New Mexico, to comply with the Americans with Disabilities Act (ADA) and make school accessible for him and others. The year he began to walk independently, he left for college in California.

Tim felt intimidated, insecure, and fearful growing up because he was small and wheelchair-bound. Putting himself out there in leadership or public speaking scared him to death. But he was learning to survive without the advantage of a bigger, mobile body. He was learning how to have influence and impact with his wit, humor, communication, message, and relationships. He was also growing in his faith in God's purpose for his life.

He worked several odd jobs throughout college, and his first career job after college was serving as the youth pastor at the church where I met him. Today, people around the country stay in contact with Tim and thank him for influencing their lives as their youth pastor, pastor, and missions leader. When I arrived at the church, Tim was transitioning from youth ministry to adult ministry, and he continued to grow spiritually, professionally, and in influence.

Two fun stories about Tim bind us together. First, Tim and his wife Kelly had chosen not to have children because his bone disease was transferable through any children they would have and tended to double in severity from one generation to the next. His father had it, but only about half as bad. So, Tim and Kelly wanted to adopt. However, they struggled to find an adoption opportunity that would work for them. One of my first actions as the new church pastor was to call the whole church to pray for God to open the doors for them to adopt, and we took up an offering to help them with adoption costs. After several false starts, the real opportunity came through, and they adopted two beautiful baby twin girls. They are now beautiful young women, wives, and mothers, and love their mom and dad very much.

Second, I had invited my father, who was a pastor, to come speak for our church. He and my mother had lived in Roswell, New Mexico, early in their marriage, and they started going to a church that God used to call them into pastoral ministry. After seeing Tim and realizing who he was, he said, "Tim's grandfather was the one who invited us to their church one day when he saw me working on a telephone connection box. And that church changed our lives. We wouldn't be here today, and my son would not be pastoring this church if it were not for Tim's grandfather's invitation for us to visit their church." Tim and I had never heard that story, and it was great to hear how God had been working before we were even born to weave our stories and callings together for his greater purposes.

Tim has a beautiful calling. As I write this, he is in the middle of a three-week mission trip to the Philippines with leaders from the U.S. missions organization One Mission Society and the Filipino denomination Faith Evangelical Church of the Philippines to help them develop their economic sustainability in the Philippines and across Asia. They are very aggressive in evangelism and disciple-making, but they realize they must grow their economic sustainability to keep their part of the Christian mission growing. Tim has the right combination of teaching, leadership, and relational skills to help our organization be a great partner with them for this purpose.

Tim and I are not the only ones with a calling from God. You are, too, and there are several things I want you to know about your calling.

FIRST, GOD CREATED YOU FOR A PURPOSE

First, God created you for a purpose. God is a being of infinite wisdom, purpose, and order. He created you in his image, with a unique design and path, to fulfill a unique purpose that fits within the overall purpose of his eternal kingdom.

The Bible expressly says in Ephesians 2:10, "For we are God's workmanship, created in Christ Jesus to do good works, which God prepared in advance for us to do." This is not a generic calling of all people to a generic list of good works. This is God's specific calling on your life, in advance of your birth—and really in advance of creation itself, for the purpose he has for your life.

Jeremiah said, "The word of the Lord came to me, saying, 'Before I formed you in the womb I knew you, before you were born I set you apart; I appointed you as a prophet to the nations'" (Jeremiah 1:4-5).

The Bible is full of people's life stories, from Adam to Noah, Abraham to Joseph, Moses to Rahab, David to Ruth, Esther to Mary, and Jesus and Paul, to name just a few. The theme of every life story in the Bible is that God had created them for a purpose before they were born, and he worked out their purpose as they followed him by faith. Your story is not in the Bible, but it is written in God's record books in heaven, and he wants us to read the Bible stories to grow our faith in his purpose in our stories now.

When I say purpose, I don't mean one single act that you will do and be finished with your purpose. I mean the whole body of outcomes created by your existence, relationships, activities, and work. Most people who seek to follow God's purpose for their lives pursue many things, but they often discover a common theme of what good their lives tend to create. They keep returning to their God-given talents, interests, and values.

God's purposes for his people are as unique and varied as the world's needs. Your calling fits somewhere in his plan. Tim's calling is developing leaders. My calling is thought leadership to transform people's lives. My wife's calling is family ties, friendships, and artistic beauty. Kelly, Tim's wife, has a calling of leadership in helping special needs kids. In recent years, they have adopted two young special needs children.

So, please be encouraged no matter how difficult your life has been. God is at work and has created you for a good purpose. Let me call you to have faith in this biblical promise.

SECOND, GOD DESIGNED YOU FOR YOUR PURPOSE

God doesn't just *create* you for a purpose; he also *designs* you for that purpose.

Have you ever wondered why you felt so different than other people? So odd and maybe even weird? I have felt that a lot. I am highly introverted, and I like to hyperfocus on specific ideas and tasks. I like gathering, developing, and communicating transformational ideas that change people's lives. I hate to do maintenance and management work. I love the development curve of taking a big idea and making it a big organization or movement. I am usually the first to leave a gathering or a party unless I hosted it for something important to my purpose. My life's work is a cycle of solitude to do the deep work of thinking, reading, and writing, followed by sharing key ideas with others in speaking, consulting, or coaching. After I have been out with people for a while, I can physically feel the serotonin (happy chemicals) in my brain disappear like they were eaten up. I feel like I have internal brain damage that is only healed with sleep and solitude. So, I am an odd duck. I am horrible at most jobs in the long run. But I am well-designed for my calling. And for that, I thank God.

The first and most important aspect of your divine design is your desires. They are the "Why" of your calling. No one will fully understand why you want certain things, not even you, and certainly not your parents. They probably love you, but they are not you, and they can't quite get you because you are your own person with your own God-wired desires. Your desire for experiences and accomplishments is one of the strongest forces that lead you toward them. It's like the salmon's urge to swim upstream to spawn or the bird dog's passion to find, point, flush, and retrieve birds. It fulfills you at a level you can't even fully explain. Look through this list of categories of things you could desire, and for each one, write down the things you love or would love.

- Interests
- Activities
- Experiences
- People
- Places
- Things
- Ideas
- Achievements
- Outcomes

What you love in these categories is a pretty good start to understanding your God-given desires, except for any that might be sin. Sometimes, our hearts can be so subtle that we are unsure if our desires are righteous or sinful. For example, you may want to excel at a sport, but you are not sure if your desire is from a pure motivation to love the sport and do well in it or if it is from an ego of pride or arrogance or insecurity that needs to be dealt with at deeper levels in your spiritual and emotional growth.

Proverbs 34:7 (NASB) says, "Delight yourself in the Lord, and he will give you the desires of your heart." I believe this means that when we grow in our love for and pursuit of God first, he clears out the sinful and false desires of our hearts and leads us to the true and righteous desires that he has wired inside of us, and he fulfills those desires by how he leads us, by his providence and by his blessings.

Philippians 2:12b-13 says, "…continue to work out your salvation with fear and trembling, for it is God who works in you to will and to act according to his good purpose." This is saying that God works in us to give us the holy will or desire to fulfill his calling.

The second aspect of your divine design is your talents. They are the "What" of your calling. They are the relationships, activities, work, and creation you can do well because they come to you naturally. The Bible calls them your gifts because God gave them to you. The Bible stories are told with the assumption that the actors in the stories have their unique God-given callings and gifts.

You can get better as you use your talents. What's important is that within these gifts lie the most important and powerful activities you can do to fulfill your calling. I think some people are primarily people-people, some are thing-people, some are idea-people, and some are process-people. That doesn't mean you can't have talent in all three areas, but often people have their primary area of strength in one of these. I'm an idea person. I thrive on transformational thought leadership, but I also like physical projects like building things and good relationships with family, friends, and colleagues. My wife is a people person. She thrives on good relationships with family and friends, but she also likes beauty and art, which she pursues through photography and painting. My father-in-law was a thing person; he was an engineer, a pilot, and an excellent mechanic. He thrived on working on engineering projects, airplanes, and cars, but he also loved good relationships and good ideas. You might take these three categories and pick which one is your first strength, then list several activities, kinds of work, or kinds of creation you love to do in that category. That might reveal some of your better talents:

- People
- Things
- Ideas
- Processes

The third aspect of your divine design is your temperament. It is the "how" of your calling. Your temperament is your personality style. It is how you do you, how you get stuff done, how you relate to people, how you use your brain and your body, how you relate to the physical world, how you relate to yourself, and how you get energized.

There are different temperament, personality, or psychometric tests you can take to understand yourself better, but for our purposes here, I would ask you to answer the question, "How do you like to live and work?" If you are as thorough and accurate as possible, you will have a pretty good read on your personality. The longer you live and the more you keep answering this question, the better you will understand your temperament. I'm convinced your core temperament is not chosen but is hard-wired. It is God-given, and working with it, not against it, is part of your calling.

My wife and I often comment on how we like to see successful oddballs. They love God, dress like they want, work like they want, make enough for their life and calling, bless others, make the world better, and are happy as clams. This is refreshing because, in a world where most people feel they must conform to outside pressures instead of pursuing their callings, it reminds us that God uniquely designs us all for our unique callings.

To understand how God has designed you for your calling, combine these three aspects: What are your strongest desires? What are your best talents? How do you like to live and get things done? Where these three aspects of your divine design come together is where God has designed you for your calling.

THIRD, GOD PREPARES YOU FOR YOUR PURPOSE

This is one of the great themes of the Bible. God prepared Moses for his calling to deliver Israel from slavery in Egypt so they could become a new nation on the frontier of their Promised Land. God prepared Moses for forty years as a prince in Egypt, but that ended in failure. Yet it was preparation. He then continued to prepare him as a shepherd on the back side of the desert for another forty years, ending in him being unknown, isolated, and irrelevant. Yet it was preparation. Then God called him at eighty to go confront Pharoah and lead Israel out of Egypt and through their forty-year sojourn in the desert right up to their entrance into their Promised Land.

God prepares each of his people for their callings, and he has been preparing you for yours. He has been making you deeper in your spirit, softer in your heart, stronger in your faith, more skilled in your talents, more knowledgeable in your field, and clearer in your calling.

FOURTH, GOD CALLS YOU TO YOUR PURPOSE

Your life purpose is called your *calling* because God calls you to it. He calls you through the inner voice of his Holy Spirit in several ways. He keeps bringing you back to the desire, talents, and temperament he gave you. He keeps bringing up the circumstances, people, problems, and opportunities he has placed you in with a sense of purpose within them. And he keeps bringing a vision back to your heart and mind about what you would do with your life if you had the faith to do so. The more you make your pursuit and love of God the priority of your life, the more God's Spirit speaks to your heart to call you to his purpose.

I often say that when God is trying to call you to do something, he doesn't quit. You may put him off for a while, but when you get serious and quiet with him again in your heart, he brings it back up.

That's how God led me in my first season of calling to be a pastor. He wouldn't quit. After thirty years of serving as a pastor, that is how God led me in my second season of calling as an international nonprofit ministry leader. He wouldn't quit.

I had a comfortable, respectable, predictable, and financially stable life as the pastor of a good church. We loved our people, and they loved us. But he would not quit calling me to the work of capitalizing the Global Church with the Spirit of Creation to save souls, solve poverty, and redeem cultures.

As I considered this new calling, all I could feel was fear. The picture I kept seeing in my mind was that if I answered this call, I would be financially driving my family off a cliff. But God wouldn't quit.

So, with fear and trembling, in my late fifties, I said yes.

I am sixty-four now, and we have been doing this full-time for five and a half years. We have not gone broke yet. God has met our needs so far. We don't have the financial margin to feel comfortable again yet. We have personal desires we can't yet fund. We have organizational programs and needs that we can't fully fund yet. We have staff that we need to hire, but we can't afford them yet. So, we are still living by faith weekly in the entrepreneurial start-up phase of this calling. Other people my age are retiring or preparing for it. I am working toward the vision of our organization empowering a million people by 2030, ten million by 2040, and a hundred million by 2050. There is no end to the work of my calling in sight. I know an end will come, and there will have to be a succession for a younger person to become the top leader of PPI. I'm hoping to pass off the top executive role at some point and move over to a role of writing and speaking after that. I hope PPI stays on track to reach its vision through 2050, whether I live that long or not. I will be 90 in 2050. I would love for God to give me longevity and to be able to celebrate that victory, but if not, I hope to celebrate it from heaven.

For now, PPI is working in seven African countries, with doors opening for our trainers to move into new countries across that continent. We are in six regions of the Philippines, with doors opening up in other Asian countries. We are in Central America and the Caribbean, with more open doors in those regions. We have strategies to reach our vision globally by leading Christian leaders to capitalize the global church. We target church, ministry, educational, denominational, and missions leaders, and we are developing key tools for them to spread this movement, like college and seminary courses, a K-12 curriculum, small group courses, and online master classes.

God led my wife and me to move to the Dallas area three years ago. We wanted to be closer to some of our children and grandchildren, and I wanted to be in the DFW area for easier access to international travel and greater access to potential Christian partners who could join the work of PPI. Connecting with potential partners for PPI has been very slow, but we are on the verge of an exciting partnership with an organization that could help us scale PPI to a whole new level to reach our vision. God willing, that will be fruitful.

That is our calling, and I bet you are glad it is not yours. But that is okay. I love my calling because God created me for it, designed me for it, prepared me for it, and called me to it. I just want God to do more than we ask or imagine to grow his kingdom through our obedience to his call. And here is the good news. You will love your calling, too. It will take faith, but God will work out his purposes and grow his kingdom through your obedience.

FIFTH, YOU ARE CALLED BEYOND YOUR LIMITING BELIEFS

My colleague, Tim, often tells people God calls us to live beyond our limiting beliefs. Most people don't answer God's call because they listen to the wrong voices of fear in their minds, repeating their limiting beliefs. Tim has overcome some limiting beliefs to answer his call to develop leaders worldwide. He teaches others to overcome these limiting beliefs:

- The Scarcity Mindset: There's not enough.
- Insecurity: I am not enough.
- Powerlessness: I can't do this.

The scarcity mindset says, "There is not enough." It fears taking a risk of using one's limited time, energy, or money. Tim recounts how every major move in his and Kelly's lives to follow their calling has caused them to face major financial risks. These include attending college to prepare for ministry, adopting two baby girls, moving to Canada to start a new church, stepping beyond the church to do workforce training in businesses, raising funds, and joining PPI to serve a global mission. He also recounts how every step of faith in his calling led him to financial rewards and rewards in relationships and achievements.

Insecurity is the limiting belief that says, "I am not enough." It says we are not smart enough, strong enough, talented enough, or good enough. It says I just don't have what it takes to do the things I wish I could.

Tim's days of being the kid in the wheelchair and being the smallest one challenged his heart and mind with thoughts of insecurity. God was calling him to a life of leadership and public speaking, but it scared him to death. But he moved forward in faith in God's call and put himself out there. So many are glad he did. He says, "Insecurity is just as strong of a barrier in people's minds as the wheelchair was to me. But we can't let our challenges define us with insecurity. Who we are must be defined by God's purpose for us, not our limiting beliefs."

Powerlessness is the limiting belief that says, "I can't do this." When faced with a problem, a challenge, or an opportunity, it makes us think and say, "I am not strong enough," "This is too much for me," or "I am too old or too young for this,", or "I just don't have what it takes."

Here is how Tim says it.

Do I still have the bone disease? Yes. Has it limited me physically? Yes. Do I have physical weaknesses because of it? Yes. Do I remember the pain and suffering? Yes. Does that mean I'm powerless? No.

I am not powerless. We are not powerless. We are not damsels in distress. We are not timid little children hiding from the school bully. We all have limitations, yes. But that does not mean that we are powerless.

Please hear my words. If you are a follower of Christ, if you have His Word, if you have been redeemed by His grace, and if you have been infused with His Spirit, you are not powerless. We are not powerless.

When I start feeling like the Goliath of limiting beliefs might be winning the battle in my mind, I read these four statements of truth and preach them to myself as often as I need:

1. *God created you with free will.*
2. *God's purpose for your life is greater than your pain.*
3. *God wants to recycle your pain for the benefit of other people.*
4. *You have a choice.*[4]

SIXTH, THE SPIRIT OF CREATION EXISTS TO FUND YOUR PURPOSE

The Spirit of Creation is not about materialism or hedonism but about kingdom-ism. It is about funding your life and calling so you can be part of the mission to grow Christ's kingdom. The philosophy that he who dies with the most toys or the most thrilling experiences is dead wrong because he who dies is dead. And after death, the Bible says, comes the judgment whose fruits last forever (Hebrews 9:27).

Pursuing God and his purpose for our lives is our most important thing because it pays us back in unimaginable rewards forever, whereas materialism and hedonism disappear in a heartbeat (Matthew 6:19-21). I'm not saying it is a sin to enjoy some nice things or experiences in this life. Of course not. God created this place for our use and enjoyment (I Timothy 6:17). I am saying we have to live with the right priorities, and the first priority is Christ and his kingdom.

God gave us the material and temporal methods of The Spirit of Creation to fund our lives and callings, which touch and extend into our eternity with him, the holy angels, and all of God's people from history.

The Spirit of Creation is God's plan to resource our lives to grow his kingdom on earth, which is part of his eternal kingdom. This is holy business dressed in work clothes.

In Chapter 14, *Fund Your Calling*, we will specifically address how to fund your calling with The Spirit of Creation and the Three Wealth Engines. For now, our purpose is to make the case that you have a calling, that it takes material resources to fulfill it, and that God gives us the principles and practices to create those resources. The Spirit of Creation is the way to fund and fulfill your life purpose.

SUMMARY

We have spent the first three chapters of this book laying a theological foundation for the Spirit of Creation. They are a theology of his kingdom, truth, and calling.

God's kingdom exists wherever His will is done.

God's truth is all truth.

God's calling is the purpose for which He created you.

The Spirit of Creation serves God's kingdom, is based on His truth, and funds His calling on your life.

In the next part of this book, I will teach the principles and practices of the Three Biblical Wealth Engines. Knowing and practicing them are the core of the Spirit of Creation. They are the root cause of human flourishing; if neglected, they become the root cause of poverty.

Chapter Four
The Three Biblical Wealth Engines

SHE ROSE BEFORE SUNRISE, WORRIED she had overslept. Since her mother had died, eight-year-old Maddo (pronounced *Mah Doo*) had essentially become the domestic slave of her oppressive father in a village in western Kenya. She had to care for him and her siblings. She would rise early to fetch water and firewood and prepare hot water and porridge so everyone could clean up and eat breakfast to start their day.

Maddo's school was in session mornings, afternoons, and evenings. At lunch and dinner, she had to come home and go through the routine of fetching water and firewood again to cook for her family. When she was late to school, she received a beating with a cane rod. So, she often skipped school to avoid the beatings.

Despite these things, she was smart, she got good grades, and she was able to attend college. However, in Kenya, good-paying jobs are few and hard to come by, even for college graduates. So, she struggled to find a way to use her abilities to create enough for her life and what mattered to her. Then she got a glimmer of how it's done with the Three Biblical Wealth Engines.

In 2012, I taught a group about the Three Biblical Wealth Engines in the city of Kisumu in western Kenya. Maddo and her husband, Jared, were hosting a team from our church who were there to do missions work and economic development. Maddo wanted to attend this training, but she supervised a group of women preparing lunch for the large crowd.

She got a copy of the training notes and studied the Three Biblical Wealth Engines, which we summarized in three words: CREATE, OWN, and GROW. She focused on applying each one as best she could, which changed her life.

First, she rented a little building with a kitchen and started a café. She had led groups of women for most of her life in feeding groups of people, and this was a way to use that ability. Soon after, she started buying catering equipment and grew a catering business for weddings, funerals, and special events in her community. For one large political event, she fed 5,000 people. I have worked in the food and beverage industry and know how hard it is to feed 500 people. So, I often say when I tell Maddo's story that I only know of two people who could feed 5,000, and Maddo is one of them.

She then partnered with some of her family to build a guest house for tourists and missions teams in the village of Ahero, just east of Kisumu. A guest house serves these travelers as a hotel and restaurant.

She also bought into a health supplement business and recruited a crew of young people to be her sales team.

Several years ago, her brother-in-law sent me an email telling me how she had bought a piece of property as an investment and then a car. He emphasized that she didn't ask her husband for money because she had her own. He thought that was funny. It is funny because it is so rare in the developing world. But mostly, it is inspiring. In 2020, I visited the Kisumu and Ahero areas to train Maddo's staff, and I rode around with Maddo in her used Toyota SUV. It was like riding around with a celebrity. Everyone knows her and looks up to her as a picture of empowerment.

She also partnered with one of her health supplement salesmen to buy a piece of agricultural land as a business. They hire workers to plant, cultivate, and harvest their crops, and they make a profit. The land gives them some equity and potential for even better and higher use as the surrounding community grows.

In 2022, I did some training for a group of sharp young people at MOI University in downtown Nairobi, Kenya. Maddo was one of the speakers. She told her story, and as I listened, I thought I heard her say her goal was to own a four-star hotel in Kisumu. So, afterward, I asked her if I had heard her correctly. She said, "Yes . . . and I will." I said, "I believe you." And I teased her, saying, "I am going to come and stay at your hotel, and I am going to call down to the front desk and complain about everything." "Oh, we will be ready for you," she teased back.

In mid-2023, I met with Maddo to coach her on her desire to develop a resort hotel in western Kenya. I advised her to buy the best property she could at the best price that could eventually fulfill her vision. I encouraged her to build the first simple structure on the property that would allow her to run some income business on the property and then to build different phases of her plan to grow the income of the property and the business. I corresponded with her in early 2024, and she said, "I have already purchased the property, and it is connected to more property that I may be able to buy in the future."

One more inspiring thing about Maddo is how she and her husband support ministries and some orphans in Kenya. She has not officially adopted those orphans, but she calls them her children, and they provide for their needs and education. Maddo and Jared have two children of their own, a son and a daughter, and with their extended "family," they are creating a beautiful legacy.

Maddo and Jared create enough for their callings to bless many. They do so by applying the Three Biblical Wealth Engines.

These principles work in the cities and villages of Kenya, Latin America, and western metroplexes like Dallas, Texas. They work wherever people have enough freedom, understanding, and motivation to apply them.

The economic and spiritual power of these three economic engines came to me in some *aha*! moments.

MY AHA! MOMENTS OF THE POWER OF THE THREE WEALTH ENGINES

I have spent my life in pastoral ministry, nonprofit work, and business. I have also spent my life trying to answer some very big questions to satisfy my spirit and mind and to benefit others.

My primary areas of research have been theology, leadership, and economics.

One of the major topics I have pursued is the answers to what causes poverty and prosperity. That question has plagued me since I was a boy visiting the third world of Juarez, Mexico, with my parents in the 1960s. That question kept growing as God took me on a journey to some of the poorest cities, villages, and slums of Africa, Asia, Latin America, and the Caribbean.

After years of research and practical fieldwork, I concluded that three core economic principles summarize the core causes of poverty and prosperity. That was my first *aha*!

Then I had an epiphany. It dawned on me that these three core economic principles that hold so much power over the human condition are taught in the Bible! In fact, the first principle is taught in the first chapter of the Bible in the creation story. And the other two are taught in the first book of the Bible. The rest of the Bible reinforces and reaffirms these foundational principles. God gave these principles so his people in this material world could live in peace and prosperity rather than insecurity and poverty. That was my major, *aha*!

I have always liked economics because of its logic, symmetry, and broad implications, but I have loved the Bible because of the power of God's truth to save our souls, change lives, and redeem cultures. Seeing these truths align from biblical and economic sources grabbed my soul because it spoke to my calling and the problems I feel compelled to help solve.

In Chapter Two, we made the case that all truth is God's truth. I see this in these three economic principles. It's an aha! that can bless your life.

To prepare you for learning and applying the Three Biblical Wealth Engines, let's start with six truths about them.

SIX TRUTHS ABOUT THE THREE BIBLICAL WEALTH ENGINES

1. The three wealth engines are cumulative in their effect.

As you apply the first one, it increases your capacity and opportunity to apply the second. Applying the first and the second increases your capacity and opportunity to apply the third. When you apply all three, they maximize your true prosperity.

2. The three wealth engines create a virtuous cycle of prosperity.

A virtuous cycle is a series of steps or actions that build strength and value, which can then be repeated to create even more strength and value. For example, eating healthy and getting good exercise create mental and physical strength and value, which is repeated to create even more. Likewise, using the three wealth engines creates economic strength and value, which can be repeated to create even more.

A vicious cycle is the opposite. It is a series of steps or actions that destroy strength and value and then repeat to destroy even more strength and value. An example is eating poorly and not exercising. That tends to damage our strength and health, and repeating it causes more damage. Likewise, neglecting the three wealth engines leaves us in a state of not having enough, and even worse, it can cause us to have less and less as each cycle of neglect spirals downward.

The virtuous cycle of the Three Biblical Wealth Engines can also build economic strength and value in your family from one generation to the other. One generation can use them and grow in prosperity, then teach the next generation how to do the same, and that generation can create even greater prosperity.

3. The Three Biblical Wealth Engines are a secret to most people.

Most people apply only one or two wealth engines but don't understand their potential, how they work together, and how to get the most out of them. Imagine a boat with one or two motors running on only half their cylinders or capacities. In contrast, the wealthy of the world use all three engines, and they do their best to use their full potential. The wealthy of the world are in on the secret, and you can be in on it also.

4. The Three Biblical Wealth Engines are based on three timeless principles.

Principles are universal laws of cause and effect. They determine that some actions always cause a certain effect. For example, the law of gravity is a universal principle. It determines that smaller things are attracted to larger things in a system where gravity exists, like on Earth. We can't just jump up and float around. We always get pulled back down by gravity.

When I was a boy, I tested this. I jumped off the roof of our house with an umbrella, expecting to do a Mary Poppins flight. However, I hit the ground immediately, feet first, in a crouch. The fall made me hit my mouth on my knees, and I came up with a bloody mouth. I was lucky it didn't knock out some of my teeth. The principle of gravity can be brutal.

I haven't needed to test that again because many experiences in my life have taught me that the principle of gravity is at work on Earth. In the same way, the Three Biblical Wealth Engines are a cause-and-effect system. To achieve true prosperity, we must start with its causes and apply them.

Since these wealth engines are based on principles, they always work in all places and with all people as long as there is enough freedom to apply them. Where they do not have freedom, people must work to gain it, or they will never have true prosperity. So, we confidently teach these wealth engines to people everywhere at all socio-economic levels. They work for the poor, the middle class, and the rich. It amazes me how I can teach the same principles to the poor in a remote village in Tanzania or to a group of businesspeople in Dallas, Texas, and they both get some key ahas! to improve their economic lives. Where people live under tyranny, we teach them to use the wealth engines as much as they can and to fight for freedom so they can use them even more to create true prosperity.

5. The Three Wealth Engines are not ideas of financial management.

The Three Biblical Wealth Engines are not ideas of financial management but principles of economics. So, what's the difference? Good financial management practices flow from sound economics, so we advocate for good financial management, but this is not a book on financial management. This is a book on how to manage the "household," or the business of your whole life. This book is a theology of economics. It is a theology of how sound economics is essential to human flourishing.

The word economics comes from the Greek word *economos*, which means household rule or management. It comes from the ancient system, in which most wealthy households had a business integrated with the family system. They may have worked in agriculture, the trades, crafts, or as merchants. Their work, workers, business, money, property, livestock, equipment, supplies, business expenses, and household expenses were all integrated into one system. How they ran it was their *economos*. Most wealthy people grew up in their family *economos* and learned it, and it became their *economos*. Theologians also refer to God's system of managing all things, which is his household, as his economy. It is his system of running all things by his truths.

So, it is in this sense that this book is about your *economos*. It is about your economic system to manage the household or business of your whole life. This is not a book on financial management. There are already plenty of great resources on that topic, and we agree with the best practices of good financial management, like eliminating consumer debt, budgeting, saving, and investing. Those are important financial ideas, verbs, and actions. This book, however, is about the economic verb of *creating*. It is how we can *create* true prosperity. This is about the *Spirit of Creation*.

6. The Three Biblical Wealth Engines are the foundation of The Spirit of Creation: the economic worldview that empowers people to flourish.

The Three Biblical Wealth Engines are the foundation of the Spirit of Creation. They are the roots of the Tree of Life. They are the economic worldview that empowers people to flourish.

Let me introduce the illustration of the Three Biblical Wealth Engines.

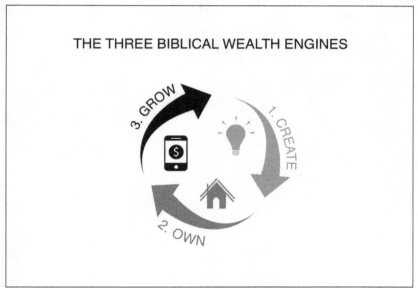

The Three Biblical Wealth Engines

In the diagram, wealth engine #1, CREATE, is pictured with the icon of a light bulb because it represents our work to create value. All work is problem-solving, and all problem-solving is a mental function of ideation and creativity. The light goes on as we work mentally to solve problems that create new value. Whether our work is more physical or mental, our primary work is using our minds to decide how to get our work done in the best way possible.

Wealth engine #2, OWN, is pictured with the icon of a house. Owning property legally is essential to creating wealth, and owning your home is usually the first and most efficient way to start owning property.

Wealth engine #3, GROW, is pictured with the icon of a phone with a payment app, as phones are often our first and most used business tool to connect with and pay others while doing business. This step is growing businesses that can multiply value. And, of course, all three wealth engines are pictured as a virtuous cycle that gets stronger with each step and activity cycle.

The next chapter will start with Wealth Engine #1 CREATE. It is the first and most important economic principle. Grasping its power can change your life.

Here we go.

Chapter Five
Wealth Engine #1 CREATE:
Value is Created

I HAD A BUSLOAD OF hungry teenagers on a freeway in Southern California. Then I saw an In-N-Out Burger.

Years ago, I was a youth pastor at Cielo Vista Baptist Church in El Paso, Texas, and we had taken some of our youth group to California to attend a week-long camp at Hume Lake Christian Camp. We had planned a few extra days to play at the beach and visit a couple of the area theme parks. It was a dream trip for many of our teens, but at this point, they were hungry, hot, and grouchy—what people now call "hangry."

It was lunchtime, and the In-N-Out was getting slammed. So, I went in first to talk to the manager to see if they could handle a busload of teenagers.

"Yes," he said, "but first, let me get my people ready."

I asked one of my helpers to tell everyone to stay on the bus, and we would go into the restaurant in a few minutes. Meanwhile, I was curious to see what the manager would do.

"Hey everybody," he shouted to everyone, the customers and his staff alike, "We are going to feed a busload of teenagers in a minute, and I need your help so everyone gets taken care of."

He then asked his regular customers who needed to order to use two designated lines, and he created a new designated order line for us.

Then, he told his team to gather around him. He told them they had the challenge of feeding a busload of hungry teenagers and serving their regular customers well. He told them he knew they could do it. Then, he began giving them assignments. Some were to load up the grill with burgers. Others were to max out the fryers. Others were to get the most common drinks iced, poured, and ready to go. Others were to take the orders and the payment accurately and quickly.

"We are going to take care of everyone," he said. "We are going to do it well. And we are going to do it quickly. Everyone put your hands in here and say, 'Go team!' on three."

And they all said, "Go, team!"

That manager inspired me. He quickly fed our kids and their regular customers with good food and a great attitude, impressing everyone with the value he created in that situation.

I don't know what happened to that young manager, but I suspect he kept that attitude of creating value in his work, and it led him to have a very successful career and life. At the time, I knew I liked what I saw in him, but I didn't know just how powerful it was. Now, I know he had the *Spirit of Creation*. He was using the first wealth engine. He was creating the best value he could.

THE PRINCIPLE OF WEALTH ENGINE #1: CREATE

The first Wealth Engine to fund everything that matters is also the most basic economic principle, and we call it CREATE. The statement of this economic principle of CREATE is this: *Value is created*. That may not sound profound, but trust me, it is revolutionary because it teaches us the true birthplace of money. Money, income, wealth, and the resources we need for our lives and everything that matters are created. It comes into existence whenever and wherever we create value.

Unfortunately, most people do not understand this. Many think that money and wealth are mysterious things that either just exist in the world or that are created somehow by the government or big corporations, and somehow some of it trickles down to us, and that the powerful people of the world determine who gets how much of it. They feel helpless in changing their economic situation. They feel doomed to just work a job with minimum prospects and minimum pressure, with enough effort to get by and not get fired, and they complain about how the system is keeping them down without fair pay or a livable wage. They are susceptible to the many politicians who affirm their feelings and promise to give them more of what they deserve from the coffers of the government, which they falsely portray as endless if they vote for them.

They believe the rich are rich because they are lucky or corrupt people who have stolen their wealth from the poor and that the poor will always be poor. So, they see no pathway upward to create a greater life.

Yes, there is corruption in this world. Yes, some are far luckier and more privileged than others. And yes, the powerful control many economic things in this world. But the most basic and powerful economic truth is not the truth of corruption, privilege, or power. It is the truth that *value is created*. And, armed with that truth, we can change our lives and fund the things that matter most.

It empowers us because God has empowered us with his image, our talents and capabilities, interests, and a world filled with needs and opportunities where we can create value—which is the creation of money—to fund our lives.

The Bible and sound economics teach us that value is created and that we can change our lives and world by doing just that.

THE TIMELESS BIBLICAL TRUTH

The biblical teaching that value is created starts in the first chapter of the Bible in Genesis chapter one, and it is reaffirmed throughout. That revelation unfolds in seven big truths.

First, God is revealed as the Creator of all things. "In the beginning," the Bible begins, "God created the heavens and the earth" (Genesis 1:1). Genesis chapter one is about someone and that someone is God. The subject is God, and the predicate is what God did. One might ask, "In the beginning of what?" Saint Augustine's answer was in the beginning of time itself.[5] He saw Genesis 1:1 starting with the creation of time by a being who lives outside the constraints of time as we know it.

So, God is first revealed as the eternal, almighty being who created the universe and the earth. He was the creator of all value in its original form.

Second, God created Earth as a habitat for humanity, with people being the pinnacle of his creation. The six days of creation unfold as a progression of things created. The last thing created on day six was a man. After each day of creation, God said it was good. After the sixth day, with the creation of man, God said, "It is very good." The message is that God created the earth within the universe to be a habitat for his prized creation, people.

Third, God created people in his own image. Genesis 1:27 says, "So God created man in his own image, in the image of God he created him; male and female he created them." This is the beginning of biblical anthropology, which teaches what man is. First, he is made in the image of God. This puts man in a unique position with God, with nature, which he is called to rule, and with angels who are of a lower created order. People have a unique relationship with God as his image bearers and their creation in his image sets up the incarnation of God the Son as a man to redeem men from their sins. It also explains why he did not do the same for fallen angels.[6] They do not bear his image. People, as God's image bearers, have a uniquely high value.

Fourth, God gave people the job description to use their God-given capacities to create added value on earth. Following the statement that God created people in his image in verse 27, the next verse gives their purpose as such. Verse 27 defines human design, and verse 28 defines human purpose. It says it this way in the New King James Version,

Then God blessed them, and God said to them,
"Be fruitful and multiply;
Fill the earth and subdue it;
Have dominion over the fish of the sea, over the birds of the air,
And over every living thing that moves on the earth."

Some people read that and conclude it is saying our job description is to have babies and grow the human population on Earth. That is part of it because God values people as his image bearers. So, God loves babies because God loves and values people. And He has given us the capacity to procreate new people created in his image. They can be a blessing to the world, and they have the opportunity to become part of God's eternal family and kingdom. However, an analysis of the five imperative verbs in this blessing reveals that our job description is to create far more value than the value we create in new people. Here is a table to see those verbs, their Hebrew root words, and their expanded meanings.[7]

The Five Imperative Verbs of Genesis 1:28

English	Hebrew	Expanded Meaning
Be fruitful	*Peru*	Flourish
Multiply	*Urebu*	Become Great
Fill (the earth)	*Umilu*	Complete it
Subdue (it)	*Wekibsuha*	Conquer it
Have Dominion	*Uredu*	Rule over it

Human beings were created on earth to flourish, become great, complete it, conquer it, and rule over it using all of their God-given capacities and resources.

Said another way, God the Creator created people in his image to be creators who complete his work on earth to make it and human culture as good as possible. They are to create new value on earth through a process similar to the one God himself used to create it. They are to conceive of new products, services, and solutions in their fertile minds and then do the work to bring them into existence as new goods on earth. Don't miss that. *One of the greatest godlike characteristics God gave us was the ability to see possibilities in our minds and then do the work to create them.* In creating value, people make their livings, serve others, make the world better, and worship God.

God established the original value in creation, and he created us in His image to co-create with Him more added value to complete God's creative work on earth. As the Bible unfolds its revelation in the New Testament, we learn that it is part of how we grow the Kingdom of God on earth. It is part of how we bring about God's will "on earth as it is in heaven" (Matthew 6:10).

The Christian worldview is one of creating value and prosperity and using it for all of God's best purposes on earth. The German sociologist Max Weber called this the *Protestant Ethic and the Spirit of Capitalism* in his research in 1904. He credited it with the economic revolution that occurred in Europe from 1600 to 1900, which brought a record number of people out of poverty and into the middle class and higher.

Fifth, sin entered the world and damaged man's capacity to create value. God cursed the earth and made it a more difficult place to create value. Man fell from his innocent nature to one damaged by sin. It caused spiritual death that separated people from God and other people, which necessitates a spiritual rebirth by faith in Christ.[8] It darkened the human mind intellectually and morally, giving us an appetite for sin.[9]

We now face difficulties from nature, other people, and ourselves in creating value. We face tornadoes, floods, and attacks from animals in nature; betrayal, corruption, and war from people; and addiction, obsessions, and failures from ourselves. So, we are not saying it is easy to create value as fallen creatures in this fallen world. Yet, it still can be done. How so? The sixth and seventh truths tell us.

Sixth, although damaged, people's ability to create value was not destroyed, and history is the story of humanity's creation of a better world.

As my theology professor, Norman Geisler, used to say in class at Dallas Seminary years ago, "In the fall, the image of God in man was defaced, not erased." Our capacity to create was damaged, not destroyed. That is why many men and women have been able to create so much good over history. They can still apply much of their God-given capacities despite the difficulties in doing so. God's common grace allows fallen people to still use the asset of God's image to create good things.

Adam and Eve's first children, Cain and Abel, created value in livestock and agriculture (before Cain let envy overcome him and killed Abel).

The earliest civilization described in Genesis 4 had three major divisions of industry: agriculture, manufacturing, and art.[10] That was people working out God's image in them.

According to the ancient Jewish interpretation of Genesis 5:29, Noah invented the plow, which made him a rich man and created new wealth for the people of his day.[11] He was John Deere, who started as the inventor of a new kind of plow in his day.

Abraham, Isaac, and Jacob all became wealthy through the livestock business. Then Joseph rose from slavery to the second highest position in Egypt to save Egypt and the family of Israel from destruction from famine through wise business practices. All of this is in the first book of the Bible, Genesis. These people created great value despite the difficulties of doing so in a fallen world, with fallen people and their own sinful natures.

The progress of the world in wealth and technology from then until now is a testimony to the truth that God's image in man was not erased but defaced. We can't save ourselves from our sin; that requires salvation by grace through faith in Jesus Christ, but everyone can create value to make their living, serve others, make the world better, and obey God. And with God's grace, it gets better.

Seventh, by God's grace, he is redeeming us not only to eternal life but back to our original purpose of creating a better world. Some Christians are so focused on their own salvation and spiritual growth and the evangelism of others that they miss Christ's redemption of all things. They miss the blessing of making a better world, a significant part of their calling in Christ's kingdom.

We cited Charles Colson on this idea in Chapter One. Colson's focus was the broad idea of shaping culture with all our value-creating works. Our focus is your particular calling to create value and how that funds everything that matters. When you are redeemed in Christ, part of your redemption is a restoration back to a higher capacity to create the value God created you to create on earth. Consider the new resources you have as a value creator who is a Christian. You have:

- New spiritual life that awakens your walk with God (Ephesians 2: 1-10).
- Forgiveness of sins gives you new spiritual freedom (Ephesians 1:7).
- An awakened understanding of God's Word (I Corinthians 2:14-16).
- A renewed mind intellectually and morally (Romans 12:2).
- A path of continual personal growth (Philippians 3:13-14).
- The presence of the Holy Spirit to guide, empower, encourage, and comfort you (John 14, Romans 8, and Galatians 5:16-26).

With Christ in your life, you can grow to sin less and create more of the value you were created to create. This is the whole redemption of God of the whole person relevant to the whole world.

The Bible teaches that value is created. The biblical spirit of creation is powerful when understood and lived. It also agrees with sound economics.

SOUND ECONOMICS 101

1776 was an auspicious year. America declared independence, and Adam Smith wrote the classic economics book *An Inquiry into the Nature and Causes of the Wealth of Nations.* The opening line says, "The annual labor of every nation is the fund which originally supplies it all the necessaries and conveniences of life . . .".[12]

In this, Adam Smith said the first principle of economics is that value is created. His phrase "annual labor" means the work people do to create products, services, and solutions, and his word "fund" means money. His first phrase was that the people of a nation create the money or wealth of a nation through their value-creating work. The phrase "the wealth of nations" originally appeared in the King James Bible in Isaiah 60:5, where God promised Israel that the wealth of nations would come to the restored holy city of Jerusalem under the rule of the Messiah.

When we look at where money (or wealth) is born through the logical lens of sound economics, the answer is that it is created. It can be observed by following the money back to its origin. All money is created by a person or group working in the private sector to produce products, services, and solutions.

The person who works in the private sector receives their pay from what they produce or sell. The person who owns a business in the private sector receives their pay from the sale of what the business produces. The person who receives pay or a benefit from the government receives it from government money that was gained by taxing it from the private sector that created it. The nonprofit employee is paid with money that people gave that was made in the private sector or money that was given by government employees who were paid with money taxed from the private sector.

Are you seeing the point? All money is created when people in the private sector create the products, services, and solutions of an economy.

That is not to say that government employment is not noble. Good government service is noble. Romans 13:4 says that the magistrate is the servant of God. Good government protects the conditions where people can live peacefully and create value. However, economically, it is not the engine that creates the wealth of a community or nation. You can use your value-creation in a government job to create your income, but it is essential to understand that the government's ability to pay you comes from what it taxes from the private sector. Government is not an economic engine, but it creates or destroys the conditions under which economic engines exist and run well.

So, money is created by people who create products, services, and solutions in the private sector and people who create good government that nourishes the private sector.

The economic principle that money or value is created is seen in several ways:

- It is seen in the progress of human wealth over time as more and more value has been created.
- It is seen in the wealth of individual nations whose prosperity is directly driven by the work of their people to create value.
- It is seen in the personal wealth of those who create greater value.
- It is seen in the highest results that have eliminated poverty in modern times. It has come by empowering the poor to create greater value.

Another way to think of it economically is to ask, "From where else could come?"

FROM WHERE ELSE COULD MONEY COME? SOME FALLACIES

There are multiple fallacies of how money and wealth are created. Here are several:

- It comes from nothing. This is just absurd. It's like the atheist who believes the universe came from nothing. Some people are economic atheists. They believe money comes from nothing.
- It comes from the natural resources of a country. Natural resources are helpful, but the people of a nation have to go to work to create the value of extracting those resources and using them or selling them. And some of the wealthiest nations per capita have very few natural resources, such as Israel, Hong Kong, and Singapore. At the same time, many nations have many natural resources, but they don't extract them, use them, or sell them. Often, they let outsiders do that, and they get exploited in the process.

- It comes from the government. We have already dispelled this myth. The government gets its money by taxing those who create value in the private sector.
- It comes from printing currency. If printing currency created wealth, every nation would invest only in printing presses and crank out as much currency as possible, and all nations would be rich. The truth is that a nation needs to print enough currency to represent the wealth being created by its people. Printing too much money just dilutes the value of money. The government policy to print too much money is a policy of inflation. It is used to justify government overspending without raising taxes, but everyone has to pay through higher prices and the lower value of their money. The poor get hurt the worst because they have less margin before they go broke. That is why inflation is called the worst regressive tax.
- The newest anti-socialist president of Argentina, Javier Milei, recently said, "If printing money would end poverty, then printing diplomas would end stupidity."[13] But we know that both are false.
- It comes from government spending. Spending by itself does not create wealth; it consumes it. It is possible to spend money on things that increase the efficiency of our work to create value, and thus, it is spending money to make money. But spending by itself does not create money or wealth. And government spending is always spending the money of the people, which assumes the government is wiser at spending your money than you are, which is usually not true.
- It comes from borrowing. Borrowing money just to borrow it creates economic collapse. It is possible to borrow judiciously for things that make enough money to pay for the cost of borrowing plus create more money, such as a mortgage on a good house you can afford or a loan for a business that will succeed. However, borrowing does not create wealth. It just creates a debt.
- It comes by enforcing price controls like the minimum wage. The truth is that wages are set by the value people create. If wages are artificially set above that, employers have to increase their prices or cut their costs to afford them. The result is that people

get fired, and more people lose money. Like printing money, if minimum wages work, why not pay everyone $1,000 per hour or $2,000 per hour? Everyone could be rich no matter how little value they create at their jobs.

- It comes from taking it from those who have it and giving it to those who do not. Taking money from people who created it has a name. It is called theft. As economist Thomas Sowell has said, "What right does one person have to what another person has created?" Regardless of the morality of it, taking from some to give to others is just reshuffling the deck. It is not creating anything new. And finally, as economist Henry Hazlitt said, "We cannot distribute more wealth than is created."[14]

Since money is created when we create good products, services, and solutions, there are some significant implications we should understand. In college and seminary, I was taught that in preaching, we should not only proclaim what is true but also answer the "So What?" question. So, in each chapter that presents the Three Biblical Wealth Engines, I will give seven implications or "so what's" of each of them. Here's the first set.

THE SEVEN IMPLICATIONS OF WEALTH ENGINE #1 CREATE

1. The human economic problem is not the distribution of wealth but the creation of wealth.

The distribution of wealth does not create wealth. It just reshuffles it. Only the creation of value creates wealth. If all we do is distribute wealth, people will consume it all and die of starvation and exposure. Another way of saying it is that nothing can be distributed unless it is created. The creation of value is the root solution to the root human economic problem.

Every resource we use must be created, or at least the opportunity to use it must be created with human work. That means someone must create what you use. The law of responsibility is that you are responsible for creating what you need and want. As the Apostle Paul put it, "If anyone will not work, neither shall he eat," (II Thessalonians 3:10 KJV)) and "…each one shall carry his own load," (Galatians 6:5 NIV).

Put another way, why is anyone else responsible for creating what you use? Demanding that is to be a tyrant. Put another way, why does anyone have the right to be your tyrant and demand that you work to create what they need and want? That would be the law of irresponsibility and the theft of your freedom, time, and effort.

Of course, parents create what their children use, but their job is to lead them to a transition to responsible adulthood, to create what they need, and to create what will be needed by their children, elderly, or other dependent family members.

2. The value we create determines the income we make.

If we make enough products, services, or solutions in a week that people will pay us $100 to do that, then we earn $100 a week. If we make more or more valuable products, services, or solutions in a week that people will pay us $1,000 to do that, then we earn $1,000 a week.

Your income is not determined by what you think your value is, what you wish your value was, or what you demand of society to pay you as a matter of justice. You can't sit on a street corner, play a guitar, and sing a few days a week, especially if you are not good at it, and then get upset because the world is unfair to you and doesn't appreciate you with enough tips.

If we want to earn more income, we must create greater value. This is the economic law of cause and effect or sowing and reaping. A small cause has a small effect, and a large cause has a large effect. If you sow the seeds of low-value work, you get low-value pay. If you sow the seeds of high-value work, you get high-value pay.

So, to receive more pay, look at the value your work is creating and look for ways to create greater value. Look for what people pay more for that you could do or learn to do. That's the pathway toward more income.

3. Socialism and charity fail to solve poverty and create human flourishing because they are schemes of wealth distribution versus creation.

Socialism redistributes wealth by force from those with "too much" to those with too little. Charity does it from those who choose to give.

Different spirits drive them, but they operate by the same essential economic activity of redistribution.

There are many times that charity is appropriate, even though it does not solve poverty, and we will explain that in Chapter Seventeen: Charity, Responsibility, Empowerment, and Partnership.

Charity is an appropriate response to crises and disasters. The problem is that socialists like to make every problem a crisis and a disaster to justify socialism and then try to keep it in place. They love it because it transfers the power and money from the people to themselves as the centralized authority that controls it.

Since the human economic problem is not solved by distribution but by creation, socialism and inappropriate charity fail to solve it. Instead, they perpetuate it. In both cases, they create whole classes of people who become passive, victimized, and entitled to receive the created resources of others instead of becoming empowered to create value and wealth themselves.

4. Public policies and infrastructures should promote and protect work that creates needed products, services, and solutions.

Any government policy that pays people not to work is economically, socially, and spiritually destructive because it destroys the human calling to create value. It is anti-human. It animalizes people like zoo creatures who are fed by their owners.

Cultures that protect and promote people's opportunities to create value, produce virtuous people, and human flourishing.

5. Every organization working in the poverty space should empower the poor to create greater value.

By "poverty space" we mean all the places around the world where poverty prevails, from sub-Saharan Africa to the slums of the world to the poor inner cities of the United States. Many organizations exist for the primary purpose of alleviating the human misery and degradations of poverty. Many primarily use charity as their strategy. Those who do not empower the poor to create greater value, which creates more income, are using band-aids on the cancer of poverty. They make the patient feel better, but they don't cure poverty. The Spirit of Creation with the Three

Biblical Wealth Engines is the medicine that cures poverty. And the starting point is empowering the poor to create greater value.

The poor are not the problem. They are the solution because they are created in God's image. They have the potential to fulfill God's command to humanity and his specific calling on their lives to create value to fund their lives, bless others, and glorify God.

6. Wealth Engine #1 CREATE is the foundation of wealth creation. It supports and permeates Wealth Engines #2 OWN and #3 GROW.

In #1 CREATE, the focus is the value we create through our direct labor. In #2 OWN, the focus is the value we create through owning property. We can own property with the money we gain by creating it. Then, we preserve that value with property. In #3 GROW, the focus is the value we create through growing business. We can start businesses with money we make from Wealth Engines #1 and #2, and then through businesses, we can multiply the creation of money.

7. To flourish, we must create the best value we can.

Since value is created, the first and most important thing you can do to grow your income and wealth is to create the best value you can.

The first enemy of income and wealth is idleness and passivity. The second is doing work that is below your capability. The third is not growing your capability.

We all experience a kind of work gravity that pulls us downward toward work that is below our true capacity and calling. The force is the feeling that the lower level of work is easier, quicker, less stressful, less risky, and more urgent. The challenge for people who want to grow their incomes and wealth is to resist these forces of ease, leisure, less stress, less risk, and urgency and rise to their highest talents, desires, and calling. I am not saying to put yourself under unbearable stress in your work to make more money. I am saying to take on the challenge of your true calling, of what God has created you and is calling you to do. Challenge yourself and strive within your passion, but don't burn yourself out by workaholism or working outside your gifts and calling.

This is a constant battle for me. My family comes from a history of homesteaders who migrated to the Territory of New Mexico in the late 1800s to escape economic hardship. They had to scratch out a living in the livestock business, working for the law, sometimes even working as outlaws, and every other means they could hustle. So, physical work is part of my family culture. My father was raised in that culture and raised me with an ethic of physically working hard. I learned to lay concrete as a teenager working with my dad, building churches and homes. I contracted concrete work as one of the ways I worked my way through college. To this day, when I hear a concrete truck coming down the street, I feel a shot of adrenaline, like it's time to grab my bucket of concrete tools and jump in with the work crew. That feels like the truest virtuous work because that was my family ethic.

I fight my family culture that says physical work is virtuous and mental work like management, leadership, research, and writing is less virtuous. However, the highest value I can create within my gifts and calling is thought leadership, like *The Spirit of Creation*.

I have had to learn to push myself upward to work at my highest level of talent, gifts, and calling and to use my hobby time to do the physical work of building things.

The phrase, "create the best value *you can*," is key because your best value is unique to you. It is the best use of *your* talents and desires to create value within your environment of opportunities and problems. No one else has the exact same combination of these factors as you. That is why I have written Chapter Seven: *Ten Ways to Create the Best Value You Can*. It will give you practical steps to rise upward and create the best value you can.

Before that, we need to correct a fallacy that plagues the human mind. Economists call it the zero-sum fallacy. To get your head right about creating the best value you can, you must get this poison out of your mind.

So, let's look at the zero-sum fallacy and detox it out of our systems.

Chapter Six
The Zero-Sum Fallacy

WHEN I WAS A TEENAGER and then a college student, I could eat enormous amounts of pizza. I loved pizza. Whenever I was eating pizza with my family or friends, I always started by mentally calculating how many pieces of pizza there were, how many people there were, and how many pieces I could expect to get. I watched carefully to see who might eat less or more than expected, which affected how much I would get.

Every piece that someone else did not eat was more for me, and every piece that someone else ate was less for me. It was a zero-sum game, and I had pizza envy!

Unfortunately, I also had zero-sum thinking about life, work, and money. I thought the way to get what I wanted was to take it from others who had my piece of the money pie.

Most people think about money this way. It is their economic model. They are trapped in a mental, economic war with everyone else, trapped in zero-sum thinking, and have money envy. They believe that, like a limited amount of pizza, there is a limited amount of money in the economy that does not grow, and we are all fighting over who will get our share of it. They think that to get money, you have to take your slice of what others might get, and when others get money, they are taking away some of what you might have gotten.

Politicians talk in zero-sum language all the time to play on this ignorance and to convince people to vote for them or their policies. I just saw a quote from a former U.S. President's wife where she said, "For many to get their fair share, many others are going to have to give up some of their piece of the pie." The irony is that she and her husband became multi-millionaires with multiple multi-million-dollar properties through their political careers. I wonder how much of their piece of the pie they think they need to give up so others can have a piece of the economic pie.

It is also seen in the misguided saying, "Live simply, so others can simply live." It implies that anything I have or use takes a piece of the pie from someone who needs it. But this is false. This fallacy is called a zero-sum game or the zero-sum fallacy because many games have a winner and a loser. One person's win is another person's loss. In other words, the game does not add more value for both players. There is zero addition. The sum doesn't change. It is a zero-sum game.

When people think this way about the economy, they think that all the wealth in the world is all there ever was and all there ever will be. It is a zero-sum. They look at the piece of the money pie that others have, look at theirs, and naturally feel like it is not fair.

But this way of thinking about wealth and money is false. The truth is that new money and wealth are created daily by millions of people creating new products, services, and solutions. This is why many individuals, families, and nations have grown their wealth in tremendous ways over time. Most people in the world are far richer than people were one hundred years ago and amazingly richer than 200 years ago. How did this happen? By people taking pieces of the pie from each other? No. It came from individuals, families, businesses, and nations creating massive amounts of new products, services, and solutions.

So, when you look at the wealth of others and your own or lack of it, you may be thinking, where is my piece of the pie? The answer is that it is not in the money and wealth that others have but in the new products, services, or solutions you will create. Since you can actually create new money by your value-creating work, *your piece of the pie is the piece you will create*. Look at this illustration of Escaping Zero-Sum thinking.

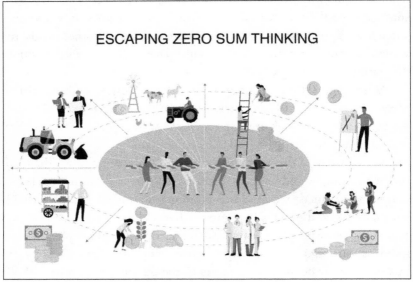

Escaping Zero Sum Thinking

Here are some key points that this diagram illustrates:

- The dark circle in the middle represents people trapped in zero-sum thinking. They think they are in a tug-of-war to *take* money from others with bigger pieces of the money pie than them.
- The people outside the dark circle represent those who have escaped zero-sum thinking and are creating new value in different sectors of the economy. Their focus is to *create it, not take it.*
- There is a ladder with a guy climbing from zero-sum thinking to value-creation thinking, or as we call it – *The Spirit of Creation.* That's what we all must do to flourish.

This means we must shift our focus from envying what others have to ambition for the value we want to create. Envy is the sinful desire for the possessions of others. Ambition is the righteous desire to create value.

Living in the zero-sum spirit of envy instead of the value-creation spirit of ambition causes all kinds of problems.

First, it creates envy, resentment, and bitterness toward anyone with more. This is one of the darkest parts of our fallen human nature. Instead of focusing on our lack of creating what we need, we would rather blame others for taking our mythical piece of the pie.

Second, it promotes corruption, lying, and theft because it makes people feel like others took their money from them or someone else, so they feel justified in taking it from others also. An example is how some justify stealing supplies, equipment, or time from their employer. They believe their employers owed it to them because they had taken it from them in the first place. They are just evening out the fair distribution of the pie. Another example is how people in some communities loot the local stores their neighbors own whenever a riot or disaster occurs. They think the store owners got what they have from stealing it from them anyway, so they will do the same thing for themselves. It all makes twisted sense if you have zero-sum thinking.

Third, it creates a spirit of passivity, victimhood, and despair. It creates the belief that the whole economic system is so rigged against us by the big, rich, and powerful forces in the world that there is no use in trying. So they don't try too hard.

Fourth, it creates a spirit of entitlement. It makes people believe they are entitled to the property of those who have more than them because they believe they stole it from them. This is the attraction of politicians who promise people they will take the property of others through taxation, regulations, policies, and government programs and redistribute it to them if they vote for them. At the global level, it is the idea that nations are poor because the rich nations have taken too much and left them without enough. Some rich nations have indeed exploited poorer nations' resources and laborers. However, when they are driven out, the economies of those poor countries often collapse because the people of those countries don't have The Spirit of Creation. They got rid of the exploiters but did not create a culture of creators.

Fifth, it gives people a false sense of how to gain what they need and want. They falsely believe the lie that the economic problem is the distribution of wealth when the truth is it is the creation of wealth. People, families, and nations do not lack what they need and want because the world's pie of wealth has not been fairly distributed. They lack it because they have not created it. There are always multiple important reasons why they have not created it. They often lack not only The Spirit of Creation but also the requisite policies and infrastructures that support it. We will address these later in Chapter Fifteen: *Solve Poverty*.

When a whole culture is corrupted by zero-sum thinking, it is doomed to perpetual economic underachievement and a commitment to false economic solutions that are all schemes to distribute the pizza more equitably rather than to create new pizzas.

One of the most important things I can teach you is to rid your mind of *zero-sum envy* and replace it with *value-creation ambition*. Stop focusing and obsessing on what others have. Those things are not yours because you have not created them. You do not have other people's houses, cars, businesses, vacations, marriages, families, nonprofits, ministries, books, boats, or anything else because you have not created them. Stop focusing on what others have. Start focusing on the value you want to create.

The human economic problem is not the *distribution* of wealth but the *creation* of wealth. Therefore, ask not what possessions you can take but what value you can create.

More than any other, this particular spirit is the hallmark of people who live with the Spirit of Creation. They are productive makers and creators. They are not focused on the possessions of others. They don't have time or mental space for envy. They accept that they don't have what others have created, so they don't worry about it. The more they mature spiritually and emotionally, the more they can be happy for those who have created wealth.

I have taught you the principle of Wealth Engine #1 CREATE: Value is Created. That truth is the basis for eliminating the zero-sum fallacy with the spirit of envy and replacing it with the righteous spirit of ambition.

Since money is created by creating value, we need to know how to create the best value we can. In the next chapter, I will teach you ten ways to do this.

Chapter Seven
Ten Ways to Create the Best Value You Can

DAVID'S STORY

David grew up in New Mexico in a hard-working family. As a teenager, he started attending our church, igniting the growth of his Spirit of Creation. He became the first in his family to go to college, and he chose New Mexico Tech, one of the country's best values for a quality engineering education.

The academic rigor of his petroleum engineering program shocked him. He had been a good student in high school, but this required a much higher level of effort and dedication. David was a high school athlete, but New Mexico Tech is known for its few athletic options and "nerd" culture. That helped him because it presented fewer distractions from classes, study groups, library time, and personal study.

David graduated and went to work in the oil and gas industry. However, unlike most new engineering students who go into oil and gas, he did not spend his new and good income on an expensive truck or lifestyle. He drove adequate used cars and saved his money for the time when he could invest it in something that could create value.

After years of working for others and learning the actual work of producing oil and gas, David was ready for his next move. He planned with several others to buy some rights to oil leases and form their own production company. He was playing golf with them when they got the call that their bid for the leases was accepted. They were excited but also scared about risking their savings. David had to have a heart-to-heart talk with his wife, saying that this venture would risk their life savings, and if they went bust, they would have to start all over again. They both agreed to go for it.

They formed their first oil and gas production company, and they made money. After a while, David's vision and his primary partner's vision for the company went in different directions, so they parted ways. David left and formed his own company with another partner in Colorado.

They developed proprietary processes and software to analyze potential oil and gas fields in Colorado and used aggressive strategies to drill and produce in them. That led them to build up and sell three oil and gas companies, one after the other. They are now on their fourth.

By the time they launched their fourth oil and gas production company, David and his partner had enough personal capital to fund it. However, the venture capital firm that had funded their previous venture called up and asked if they could fund this one, too. They agreed to it. That's pretty good when a venture capital firm comes to you and asks for the privilege of investing in your new company because you have been such a good money-maker for them.

Along the way, David invented a sports product. He launched a business around it that is now spreading through multiple sports and leagues, from high schools and colleges to professional sports. He and his wife have also invested in some properties they have developed to sell, rent, or keep.

David is a smart, hardworking, and ambitious guy, but the theme he keeps returning to is the Spirit of Creation. He lives to be a value creator, leading his companies and employees to live out the Spirit of Creation and be value creators. I have been with David several times, where he has been giving motivational public speeches about creating a personal brand and reputation as a value creator.

Not everyone has the wiring or desire to get the kind of education David got and grow businesses to the size that David has. But God has blessed us all with his calling and the capacity to create value that fits our needs and fulfills some of the world's needs, and Wealth Engine #1 Create is the place to start.

We have given you the principle, the practice, and the implications of this wealth engine. We have also warned you about the zero-sum thinking that blocks this wealth engine. Now, we will give you ten ways to create the best value you can.

Don't be overwhelmed by trying to master all ten. Focus on the one or two applications that are relevant to you now. Then, later, you can focus on others.

TEN WAYS TO CREATE THE BEST VALUE YOU CAN

1. Think of Yourself as a Value Creator.

Think of yourself as a value creator by constantly looking for what else you can do to solve the most pressing problems at your work and create the best solutions. To do that, we need to eliminate these unproductive ways of thinking about ourselves. Do not think of yourself as...

- A time spender. Don't see your value as giving your time to your job. Your time is not valuable to anyone except yourself. Prove your value by creating the best value you can quickly and effectively.
- A space taker. Don't see your value as taking up space at your work. Don't stand around, sit around, or hang around and think there is any value to it.
- A victim. Even if someone has victimized you, don't think like a victim who can't change his/her life or solve problems. Don't become paralyzed. Stay positive and seek to conquer problems and create solutions.
- A tool. Don't see yourself as a tool someone else has to use and direct. Don't wait for directions on what to do when you already see some things that need to be done. Be an initiator; do not be passive. See what needs to be done and do it.
- A role filler. Don't think that being given a role at work entitles you to the pay you want. It doesn't. Your value is only as good as the value you create in that role. If you have been assigned to supervise or manage others, give your team the best leadership you can to create great value.
- A title holder. Don't feel entitled to be paid just because you exist or because you or someone else has given you a title.

Remember, the value you create determines the money you make.

2. Raise your ambition and lower your envy.

Again, you raise one thing in your heart and mind and lower another thing by your focus. You raise the thing you choose to focus on, and you lower the thing you choose to ignore. That's why the Bible says, "Think on these things," in Philippians 4:8. Because we become the object of our focus.

So, the mental practice I encourage you to do is to make a list or create a collage of the most important kinds of values you believe God wants you to create. The problem with most dream boards is that they tend to picture materialistic goals. They are pictures of houses, cars, boats, airplanes, and exotic vacations. Let me challenge you to think higher and deeper than that. Think of how you want to help others with the value you create. It can be through business, education, nonprofit work, religious work, art, sports, government, family, or any other good work.

Elevate the value you want to create for others in your heart and mind and focus on it. Then, look dispassionately at the possessions of others with a genuine spirit of "good for them, but that is not my priority. I will gain whatever things God intends me to have as I create the value he wants me to create."

Replace zero-sum envy with value-creation ambition.

3. Raise your effort.

Often, we just need to try harder. We must stick with things longer and work with more commitment, intensity, and tenacity. I'm not advocating workaholism. I'm saying when it is time to work, give it a serious and sustained effort.

The pattern in America of those who rise out of poverty is that the first generation that pursues it works harder than most. They improve their family's position and help their children get educated. Then, their educated children leap to higher economic levels.[15] The second generation tends to work hard, but not as hard as their parents. The third generation of wealthy families often works even less. Often, wealth dissipates by the third or fourth generations, who really don't want to work at all. So, the poverty cycle starts over. They go from kings to paupers in three or four generations because they quit working hard to create value.

If you don't have the income you need or want, you may have to try harder. And teach your children to do the same.

4. Raise your people skills.

Emotional intelligence is realizing how the people around you feel and responding to them appropriately. Some come by it more naturally than others. Some are raised to be intentionally aware of what it is and to respond to it with good manners and care for others. Some are not.

It is the most missed skill and characteristic I see in people who sabotage their ability to create value. Instead of value, they create hurt, offense, and harm in their fellow workers, employees, customers, industry colleagues, and community. In contrast, it is the most common skill I see in genuinely successful people. They are the kind of people others trust and want to work with.

It starts with resolving to try to sense what others around you may feel and then responding to them with care and encouragement. Sometimes, it's good to ask someone how they feel and do your best to affirm and encourage them.

My temperament is that I tend to hyper-focus on ideas and projects, so in a work setting, I can be aloof and unfocused on others. This has been brought to my attention multiple times and I have to work at it to have better people skills. I have natural people skills as a public speaker. I can sense the emotional energy of a crowd and respond appropriately. However, I don't have natural people skills in many social settings. So, I have to work on it. Occasionally, my wife will nudge me if we are in a public setting, and I am not aware of how I am coming off. Early in our marriage, I resented it, but I have come to appreciate that she is more in tune with people's feelings and helps me.

Another simple but important habit of good manners is to acknowledge everyone in a room that you enter. Then, when you leave, say your goodbyes to everyone.

Another is to look people in the eye and acknowledge what they are saying without trying to dominate the conversation with your ideas or solutions. Even when we must correct others, as we sometimes do as managers, we should follow the biblical admonition and do so gently (Galatians 6:1).

5. Raise your vision, goals, and action plan.

It is easy to get lost by lowering our heads and our sights on the immediate tasks and problems in front of us in our jobs and our lives.

We need to lift our heads and sights and think farther ahead mentally. We need to list two or three of the most important goals of value we want to create. Then, we need to create a plan of action to get there. Then, we need to block out our calendar to work on that plan. Then, we need to discipline ourselves to do the right work when it is time to work.

When we feel lost again, we need to rinse and repeat this process. I repeat this process often to refocus my vision, goals, and action plan. Right now, I am writing on a Wednesday morning at 10:00 a.m. I have been writing since 6:30 a.m. and have blocked out time to write until about 11:30 a.m.

Here's why. My vision is to lead 1 million people to save souls, solve poverty, and change the world by 2030, 10 million by 2040, and 100 million by 2050. To do that, I must raise the financial partners to support our nonprofit organization and create the training content for those we train in the worldwide poverty space. The most powerful tool I can use to accomplish these outcomes now is to write this book and launch it as well as I can. It can create awareness in the U.S. of our work internationally and be a training tool for the people we serve. It is a strategic tool because my primary gift and calling is thought leadership, and writing books like this is a strategic way to do this. I am blocking out my morning work hours to write this book because the morning hours are my best time for mental energy and clarity to write. Writing is hard mental work, and I can only do it productively for this block of time. I will use my afternoons for less demanding tasks.

I just described how I manage my vision, goals, action plan, schedule, and actual work to create the best value possible. Now, do likewise, using your gifts to fulfill your calling.

6. Raise your integrity.

All positive and sustainable economic activity is built on trust. Your ability to rise in a career or business ownership will largely depend on your trustworthiness. Trust must exist between team members at work, businesses and customers, lenders and borrowers, government and the private sector, neighbors and friends, and spouses and family members.

All trust is based on agreements; doing what you say you will do is the essence of trustworthiness and integrity. To be promoted, land a higher job, or grow your business to a new level, you must improve your integrity and prove trustworthy.

When I was contracting concrete work in my college days, I broke trust with a builder. I implied that I would do a good job, but I got injured on the job site and did not do the job right. I should have stopped and talked it over with the builder and worked out a later time to do the job when I could do it properly or to pass it off to another contractor. But I acted against my better judgment.

I got paid, but over time, it ate me up. Months later, I went to the builder and reimbursed him for that job because he had to have it redone. He said, "Don't worry about it. I wrote that off on last year's business." I said, "I have to do this. I have to make this right. This is as much for me as it is for you."

I never contracted with that builder again, but I had made things right and knew he appreciated me for it. I heard from several others that he had told them what I had done as an example of integrity. At the time, I couldn't afford to give him that money, but I couldn't afford to be untrustworthy even more.

One of the most common problems in business is having employees with access to money or supplies steal some of it. I have friends who owned a high-end ice cream shop that nearly went out of business because the employees gave their friends so much free ice cream. I have known many business owners whose managers stole money from the cash registers. When you take on a responsibility where you have access to the business's money, supplies, and power, you are making a tacit agreement to protect the business's best interests. When you break that agreement, you can't be promoted and certainly don't have the standing to run your own business successfully. When it comes to integrity or the lack of it, we reap what we sow.

7. Raise your level of responsibility.

There are two work options: self-employment or employment by others. In each one, raising your level of responsibility raises the value you are creating, eventually raising your income. Raising your level of responsibility means raising the level of the problems which you take on to solve. All work is problem-solving, so to make more money, solve bigger problems.

Let's start with self-employment. Some choose self-employment because it best suits their nature. Others chose it because few or no good jobs suit them. The act of employing yourself is a rise in your level of responsibility. It says I will solve the problem of creating a job for myself. Self-employment work may be evident to you, or you may have to do some thought work to figure it out.

When you are choosing a self-employment option, consider several things. Consider how you can maximize your talents and desires and consider the highest needs of others. Then, start where you are and with what you have.

When God called Moses, he asked him, "What's in your hand?" (Exodus 4:2). It was a shepherd's staff, and God used it to perform miracles in Moses' role as the deliverer of Israel. The idea is that God can take what you have and use it to create much. But we have to put it to work.

So what is in your hand? What knowledge, abilities, talents, skills, strengths, desires, assets, tools, equipment, and connections do you have? And what opportunities do you see around you? What problems do people around you have that you could solve?

Often, we don't think of what we have and where we are as assets for making money. Moses didn't think much of his shepherd's staff, but God used it. Often, the most common things you have and where you live create good opportunities to make money.

Our friends, Let and Abby, in the Philippines, work for a missions organization. They created a simple coffee and pastry shop in their neighborhood to create extra income. Recently, they were looking for a new income stream. They thought of how much they love their pet dog and how much their neighbors also love their pets. They got the idea to sell pet food in their neighborhood. Now, they buy pet food in bulk from a wholesaler for one price and repackage it in smaller packages at a marked-up price to sell to their neighbors. They have created a new income stream and are also having fun meeting their neighbors. There is no telling what future opportunities they might discover from their new connections.

Another friend of mine has an online makeup instruction and sales business. Recently, she started a new venture, window cleaning. She calls her business Squeegee Girl and promotes it on social media. I love this business because it is simple to start. It is easy to get the supplies to clean windows, and there is a huge need for window cleaning where she lives.

After a day of training on the Three Wealth Engines in Malindi, Africa, one of the trainees said, "I have an acre of land that is sitting vacant and unused. I hadn't really thought of putting it to work, but I could rent it out, plant a crop, or use it in some way to make income. And I feel convicted that God wants me to put what I have to work." Indeed.

After a training conference in Guatemala, a couple who attended the training and owned a couple of clothing stores said, "We want to create our own line of clothes that we can sell to other shops throughout Guatemala." They had the talent, skills, desire, and vision for it. They needed to raise their game of solving this bigger problem.

My friend was consulting a man who started a business selling breakfast burritos out of several gas stations. His business had grown from a few burritos sold out of one gas station to many sold out of several. He was making $300,000 a year in profit. "I never knew there was so much money in burritos," my friend said. There is a lot of money that can be made by people who start where they are with what they have and then grow it as they are able.

If you choose to be employed by others, one of the most powerful ways to create the best value you can is to take on a higher level of responsibility. Solve bigger problems. If you are an entry-level worker, work with the attitude of making your team successful. If you are a supervisor, step up to manage your team well. If you manage a department, look for ways to help your fellow managers. If you are a general manager, look for ways to improve your organization's overall performance. Step up to the highest level of responsibility that fits your level of capability and desire.

When we are solving problems that are at our optimum level of capability, it feels energizing. When we work below that level, we get bored. When we work above that level, we get stressed out. So, if you are employed and have more capability to solve bigger problems with good energy, start working on the ones you know you are allowed to work on and seek permission to work on the ones, you would like to. Bosses are constantly evaluating the capability of their employees. The ones who solve the extra and higher problems are the ones who get promoted and paid more.

8. Raise your knowledge and skills.

Knowledge is what you know is true. Skills are what you can do. Every field of work has its own specialized body of knowledge and skills. Gaining more knowledge and skills in your field of work will help you create more value. You can learn it from industry resources, on-the-job training, informal learning that you pursue through books, podcasts, and online courses, and formal learning through different kinds of schools.

I learn by reading, observing others, and using quick online resources. I always have a stack of three or so books on the corner of my desk that I am reading to learn knowledge and skills in some area of my interest and work. I like to hang out with people who do the things I am interested in so I can learn from them. I use quick online resources to learn about words, concepts, people, and processes that are relevant to my work.

Let me encourage you to know your best learning style and organize your life to be a continual learner of the knowledge and skills that can help you create the best value you can.

9. Raise your stewardship.

We call giving stewardship because it recognizes that all things belong to God (Psalm 24:1) and all blessings come from God (James 1:17). So whatever God lets us possess in this life is our stewardship or management of his possessions and blessings. Raising your stewardship to give ten percent of your income or more to the ministries and causes that you believe God would have you support will raise the value you create in several ways.

First, God will bless your work and finances. Proverbs 3:9-10 says:

Honor the Lord with your wealth,
With the first fruits of all your crops;
Then your barns will be filled to overflowing,
And your vats will brim over with new wine.

I want to honor the Lord with my income and wealth because I acknowledge that it all belongs to him and that he blesses me with temporary stewardship of it. I want my barns to be overflowing, my vats to run over, my bank account to have enough, my bills to be paid, and to have food on the table.

Second, giving the first part of your income makes you a giver, and giving is the first part of being a value creator. Creating value in a free society precedes the reward you will receive from it. It is an act of faith in God and his truth that if you give, it will be given to you (Luke 6:38), and what you sow, you will reap (Galatians 6:7). The motivational Christian speaker Zig Zigler liked to say it this way, "Do more than you are paid to do, and eventually you will be paid more for what you do." Giving value first in hopes of a return is part of the Spirit of Creation.

Third, it will make you more joyful, and joyful people create more value. As Jesus said, "It is more blessed to give than to receive" (Acts 20:35).

I have lived and worked in churches, ministries, and nonprofit work for a long time, and I have known many people who were givers and many who were not. Without question, the givers were more blessed, greater value creators, and happier people.

When we live life with our hands open and upraised to God, he places more blessings in them. When we live with our hands pointed downward, clinching our possessions without a spirit of giving, we can't receive the greater things that God would have for us.

To create the best value you can, give ten percent of your income where God leads you. It will unleash your Spirit of Creation in new and better ways.

10. Raise your stake in property and business.

In Wealth Engines #2 and #3, we will flesh this out in detail, but to start you thinking in that direction, you can create the best value you can by raising your ownership in property and business.

Creating the best value you can refers mostly to the direct work you do, but your ownership of property and business creates vehicles that make money beyond your direct work. It transforms money into capital, which is money and resources that are working for you to create more value. We will explain those in more detail in the next five chapters.

SUMMARY
10 Ways to Create the Best Value You Can

1. **Think of yourself as a value creator.**
2. **Raise Your Ambition and Lower Your Envy.**
3. **Raise Your Effort.**
4. **Raise Your People Skills.**
5. **Raise Your Vision, Goals, and Action Plan.**
6. **Raise Your Integrity.**
7. **Raise Your Level of Responsibility.**
8. **Raise Your Knowledge and Skills.**
9. **Raise Your Stewardship.**
10. **Raise Your Stake in Property and Business.**

This completes the chapters about the principle, practices, implications, and applications of Wealth Engine #1 Create.

The next chapter will present Wealth Engine #2: Own. It is a powerful and important wealth engine that separates the prosperous from the poor of the world.

Chapter Eight
Wealth Engine #2 OWN: Property Preserves Value

THE BOY WITH THE BLOODIED elbow, tear-streaked face, and snotty nose stood there with his angry mother. She was showing my mother what I had done. My mom made me apologize for throwing a caliche rock at the boy. While our parents had been at church choir practice, we kids were playing caliche war on the church's vacant lot where a new building was under construction.

Caliche war was one of my favorite games as a kid. We played it in the foundation trenches of a new church building our church was building in El Paso, Texas. Just a foot or two under the sands of El Paso lies a layer of caliche, a brittle white calcium deposit from the prehistoric inland sea that had covered the area in ages past. Caliche breaks up into clods and rocks that are the perfect size for throwing at your opponents. And we perfected the art.

Winston Churchill said, "There is nothing more exhilarating than to be shot at with no result."[16] The closer an enemy rock came to hitting us, the more exciting it was. And we were trying to nail our opponents in the trenches on the other side of the property . . . for God and country.

I apologized to the boy and his mother, but I quietly considered it his risk to join the battle, and I was proud of my accurate throw. My mom didn't follow up with me for private discipline. I think she thought that the boy and his mother were overreacting over his sore arm. It was a different time.

My playgrounds as a kid and my workplaces as a young person were construction sites. The images in my mind of my dad in my youth and his young adulthood were of him building buildings. So, that's where I played, and that's where I learned to work.

My dad was a pastor, but his gifts made him a property developer for ministry. He was the leader or the co-leader of ten building projects for churches in Texas and Colorado and one for a Bible college in Mexico.

He also traded up and built houses to improve our family economy. He and the congregations he led created tens of millions of dollars of value in property now used by churches, ministries, and missions. I'm not sure he fully grasped the economic power of what he was doing. He was doing what came naturally and what seemed like the next logical step in growing ministries.

I got his DNA in this area. During my season of life as a pastor, the congregations I led acquired hundreds of acres of property and built millions of dollars in facilities for churches, schools, and ministries. Under my current leadership of People Prosper International, we have seen our trainees in the developing world buy properties and build homes and buildings for businesses, schools, medical facilities, and ministries.

My wife and I have also grown our family economy with property through trading up, flipping, developing, and owning rental properties. It's second nature for me to look for ways to use property to benefit ministries, businesses, and people economically.

J.D. Rockefeller reportedly said, "90% of wealth is made in real estate." That may be an overstatement, but a McKinsey & Company report shows that two-thirds of the wealth held in ten countries – the U.S., China, the United Kingdom, Germany, France, Canada, Mexico, Sweden, Australia, and Japan – is held in real estate.[17] Owning the best property you can is key to growing your wealth because it is rooted in the second most important principle of economic empowerment. It is the principle of Wealth Engine #2.

When you take money you have earned with your Wealth Engine #1 CREATE and use it to buy good property, your Wealth Engine #2 OWN, something magical happens. The rest of this chapter and the next two chapters will describe that magic and how to take advantage of it. Once again, here is the Three Biblical Wealth Engines illustration.

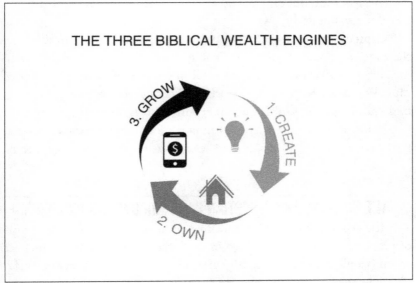

The Three Biblical Wealth Engines

THE PRINCIPLE OF WEALTH ENGINE #2 OWN

The second wealth engine of the Spirit of Creation is the second most important economic principle. We call it OWN.

The economic principle of OWN is this: *Property preserves value.*

This principle is more profound than most people realize because, without property, you do not have the best asset to keep money from disappearing. You can work as hard and as smart as you want to CREATE all the income you want, but if you don't have property, your money can easily disappear because *money has wings.* In contrast, property is here to stay and usually grows in value. The magic that happens when we buy and improve property, as Hernando DeSoto says in *The Mystery of Capital,* is that our *money turns into capital.*[18] It does not disappear. It remains and grows.

Capital is different from money. Money is the currency that you can spend easily and quickly. Money decreases in value over time through inflation. Money also disappears through spending. That is why we say money has wings. But capital, and especially capital in good property, has roots. It remains and grows.

Capital is any asset you can put to work to make money. In this case, the kind of capital is property. People usually use the word capital to mean money that funds a business. However, the five common kinds of capital or assets people put to work to make money are people, specialized knowledge and skills, equipment and supplies, property, and money.

Remember, the magic of using money we earn to buy property is that it turns our money into capital, and *capital is the engine of escaping poverty.*

THE BIBLICAL AND CHRISTIAN CASE FOR OWNING PROPERTY

The economic principle of owning property and the legal principle of property rights are also rooted in the Bible. God gave these principles so his people could have security and prosperity in this material world. God has revealed the biblical and Christian case for owning property and property rights through seven unfolding truths in the Bible.

First, God is the ultimate owner of everything because he created it. Biblical and Christian worldviews always start with theology about God himself. Psalm 24:1 says, "The earth is the Lord's and everything in it, the world, and all who live in it."

Second, in the Cultural Commission in Genesis 1:28, God gave mankind's first job description. It requires many people to own specific parts of the earth. Here again is a table to see the verbs of Genesis 1:28, their Hebrew root words, and their expanded meanings.[19]

The Five Imperative Verbs of Genesis 1:28

English	Hebrew	Expanded Meaning
Be fruitful	*Peru*	Flourish
Multiply	*Urebu*	Become Great
Fill (the earth)	*Umilu*	Complete it
Subdue (it)	*Wekibsuha*	Conquer it
Have Dominion	*Uredu*	Rule over

The fulfillment of the command to fill the earth happens at several levels. First, at the level of mankind filling the earth, then at the national, family, and personal levels to fill specific properties on earth. At the individual level, two families can't fill the same property, subdue it, and have dominion over it because they will have conflict over it. The Cultural Commission requires property ownership. It is impossible to be fruitful, multiply, fill the earth, subdue it, and have dominion over it if you don't own the land where you are doing these things because others will claim it. Property ownership settles the dispute, at least legally. This is the storyline of human history, most wars, and just about every Western movie. People struggle to gain, develop, and keep their property for security and prosperity against criminals, outlaws, enemies, and tyrants who covet and try to take it.

John Lennon romanticized the idea of no one owning property in his famous song, *Imagine*. One line says, "Imagine no possessions: I wonder if you can." Yet, in his lifetime, Lennon owned multiple multi-million-dollar properties and estates in England and America. The last one he owned and lived in at the time of his death in New York was the massive apartment in the Dakota Building in the Upper East End of New York, and it is for sale for $47.6 million.[20] It's funny how those who make a living denouncing property ownership tend to have the most of it. That's because the Second Wealth Engine is an undeniable truth.

Third, God gave his people, Israel, a specific land on earth for their security and prosperity. God told Abraham, "Leave your country, your people, and your father's household and go to a land I will show you" (Genesis 12:1). When he arrived there, he said, "To your offspring, I will give this land" (Genesis 12:7). Deuteronomy 28:11 says, "The Lord will grant you abundant prosperity – in the fruit of your womb, the young of your livestock, and the crops of your ground – in the land he swore to your forefathers to give you."

Fourth, Genesis 23 describes the legal land purchase transaction of the cave at Machpelah between Abraham and Ephron the Hittite to demonstrate righteous and legal land ownership. There was a description of the property where Abraham wanted to bury his wife, Sarah. There was the discovery of the owner. There was the discovery of the owner's willingness to sell. There was a negotiation of the price. There was an agreement to the transaction. There was the payment of the price. There were witnesses to the transaction. Abraham also received a legal deed for the property. Genesis 23 is one of the most ancient texts of history describing the transaction of real estate. It serves as a historical record and a lesson of the importance of personal and legal land ownership for purposes exclusive to owned property.

Fifth, God built individual personal property rights into the Law of Moses, Israel's constitution in the Old Testament. We see this in two places in the Ten Commandments. The eighth commandment, "You shall not steal" (Exodus 20:15), is a negative statement of a positive principle. The positive principle is that people have the right to own personal property. Stealing is not stealing if there is no ownership and everything is held in common. This commandment sets the cultural boundaries of personal property in Israel, which differed from many other tribal cultures.

The tenth commandment, "You shall not covet your neighbor's house [or other possessions]" (Exodus 20:17), is the prohibition against even envying the possessions of others. God commands his people to keep their eyes and hearts focused on their own households, businesses, work, and properties. This will prevent them from violating the sacred rights of their neighbors. You will discover that the greatest damage that others will do to you will come from them coveting and trying to take what you possess in your family, friendships, work, position, things, business, money, and property. God knows this and sets moral boundaries to protect us from doing it or being victims of it.

In Exodus 22:1-15 the Law of Moses gives guidelines for restitution if a person steals, damages, or destroys another person's personal property. In Deuteronomy 19:14, the Mosaic Law says, "Do not move your neighbor's boundary stone set up by your predecessors in the inheritance you receive in the land the Lord our God is giving you to possess." In this law, God establishes that the land ownership boundaries between neighbors are sacred. They are moral boundaries in God's eyes. This is why the modern claims that those who damage, destroy, or steal others' properties are not serious crimes because they don't hurt anybody is false. They are false because it took those people's lives to earn and develop them. The destroyers destroy the value of people's pasts and the potential of their futures when they damage, destroy, or steal their properties. Property destruction is life destruction. Only those who are morally corrupted by relativism and covetousness can deny this.

The Old Testament land of Israel was unique in that God gave specific land to specific families forever. Every fifty years, the year of Jubilee came. In the year of Jubilee, all slaves were freed, and all property sold or lost was returned to their original families (Leviticus 25:8-55). Jubilee is not practiced today in Israel, and God did not require it of other nations, but it does emphasize God's insistence that Israel in the Old Testament economy was to be a landed people and that there were to be personal sacred property rights for the families of Israel. It also teaches that families should try to grow and maintain their prosperity by passing down land ownership within their families from generation to generation. This is only possible if there is generational family continuity through a common faith in God and a commitment to faithful marriage. Two factors that destroy family wealth are sin and divorce. Because of these sins and their consequences, countless wealth and properties have been lost to families across generations.

Sixth, Christianity has championed the biblical principle of property rights. German sociologist Max Weber, in his 1904 work *The Protestant Ethic and the Spirit of Capitalism*, concluded that the preaching of Martin Luther, John Calvin, and John Wesley led others to create value, to own property, and to develop its potential to grow the kingdom of God on earth. It was the main factor that lifted millions out of poverty and into the middle class in Europe from 1600 to 1900.[21] It was the largest human movement out of poverty in human history to its date.

John Locke, the 17th-century theologian and political philosopher, was one of the most influential Christian thinkers to champion property rights. His *Two Treatises on Government* were published in 1689. It was the most comprehensive work to integrate biblical theology with political economy up to its time. His works were some of the most influential thought leadership on the United States Founding Fathers. Some of his phrases and concepts are found in the Declaration of Independence and the U.S. Constitution. His core philosophy was that God has given all people the rights of life, liberty, and property and that the purpose of Government is to serve as God's steward to protect these rights. And, when a government fails to protect these rights, it is people's God-given right to replace that government with one that will. This was revolutionary thinking, and it animated the Founding Fathers and the American colonial patriots to overthrow the abusive tyranny of England and declare America a free and sovereign nation.

Locke's chain of reasoning was this: God created people in his image with certain rights. The first is life. A person has the right to do what it takes to stay alive, work, and make a living. A person is the rightful owner of their life, body, mind, labor, and the fruits of their labor. The fruits of their labor, whether money or the possessions they buy with their money, are their property. This includes land they purchase with their labor. These are the most sacred civil rights people have, and the purpose of government is to protect them.

Locke's Christian thought leadership, which championed property rights, laid the foundation for the founding of America, which became the most powerful economic engine in human history.

Seventh, cultures with property rights and ownership have flourished while those without it have languished. Think America, Israel, and Singapore versus Cuba, Venezuela, and Haiti. The former are economic engines built on property rights, and the latter are economically struggling countries where property rights are nonexistent, difficult to gain, or diminishing.

That's the case for property rights and ownership from a biblical and Christian worldview. Now, let's look at it from the discipline of economics.

ECONOMICS 101 ON PROPERTY RIGHTS

Two major economic philosophies have competed for dominance for several hundred years. One advocates for private property ownership, and the other advocates for the collective ownership of everything, with a central government regulating it. The first advocates economic freedom and is called capitalism. The second advocates for economic control and is called socialism. We are advocating for economic freedom, including property rights. We advocate for it from logical and historical evidence.

The logical argument for the freedom to own property is that people produce much higher value when they benefit from what they create. They are free to own the fruits of their labor, the incentive for effort and innovation that moves the world forward in prosperity. When people live in a system where everyone else owns the fruits of their labor, the incentive for effort and innovation disappears, and people innovate and produce far less.

The argument from historical evidence is simple. Do people clamor to escape freedom or socialism? Do people clamor to immigrate to freedom or socialism? History is clear on this one. Even those who clamor for socialism in free societies do not leave to live in socialist countries. University academics who despise economic freedom are not going to live in China, Cuba, or Venezuela. They like the real economic benefits of freedom and the theoretical promises of socialism. The American socialist politician Bernie Sanders honeymooned in Soviet Russia but chose to live in capitalist America. In America, he had amassed a net worth by 2020 of $2.5 million through his salary as a U.S. senator, the sales of his three best-selling books to the American free market, and his three homes.[22] It turns out for Bernie that socialism is a great place to visit, but he wouldn't want to live there.

Hernando De Soto is a thought leader from Lima, Peru, who has spent his life researching and working to solve poverty and create prosperity around the globe. In his book, *The Mystery of Capital: Why Capitalism Triumphs in the West and Fails Everywhere Else*, he explains that the West is built on the culture of property ownership and rights while most of the rest of the world is not. That's why most of the rest of the world is languishing economically. He demonstrates through research and the work of changing people's opportunities and cultures to own property that the difference between the rich and the poor is that the rich legally own property and the poor do not. The world's poor live on and work on land, but they do not own it with a legal deed. That means they cannot access capital, which is the vehicle for escaping poverty.

De Soto has worked with university students studying the major slums worldwide, from Haiti to Nairobi, Cairo, and Lima. In the slums of Lima, Peru, they conducted experiments that allowed residents to own their shanties with a legal deed. Amazing things happened. The new owners started to fix them up. Some started businesses out of theirs. Some added on. Some bought others' shanties and created larger homes, businesses, or rentals. Whole neighborhoods began to improve with new services and utilities as people became interested in improving their lives by improving their properties.

What happened in those slums when people became property owners is a picture of what happens everywhere. Their prosperity increased because they engaged in the second wealth engine of OWN. They got to benefit from how property uniquely creates multiple values simultaneously. They got to turn money into capital. They participated in the Spirit of Creation.

THE UNIQUE MULTIPLE VALUE-CREATING NATURE OF PROPERTY

Property is a uniquely powerful kind of capital because it can create more kinds of value simultaneously than any other. Consider these kinds of values that can be created with property.

- A place to live.

  You must live somewhere, and you will probably have to pay to live there unless you have someone willing to provide you with housing for free. Since you will have to pay to live somewhere, you should use your housing money to buy a home.

- Peace and rest.

  Many rental housing options are not very peaceful and restful. They tend to be in nosier, more crowded, and busier places. Being at peace and being able to rest is one of the values that home ownership can provide.

- Security.

  Properties you might own tend to be in safer places with less crime and better security. It is safer to be surrounded by owners than renters. Owners create value in their homes and neighborhoods by investing in them. Renters are notorious for property damage because they don't own them. There is value in living in a more secure place.

- Storage.

  Properties you might own often have better spaces to store your possessions, from places to park vehicles to places to store equipment and other possessions. Many people who live in small rentals often rent storage spaces for some of their possessions. Using that money to buy property to store your things is better.

- Work.

  Many people do much of their work from home. My main office for PPI, for some private equity work, and my writing is in my home. The same is true of our other PPI employees and my business partners. Why pay for office space if you don't need it? Have your meetings at other people's offices, public spaces like coffee shops, or flex spaces that charge to use the space just for your meeting time. Save that money and use it to buy a home with a workspace.

- Garden.

  Depending on the size of your property, you can grow food crops on a small farm, in a large garden, in a small garden, or even in pots on your patio.

- Livestock.

  On your property, you may be able to grow chickens, goats, pigs, cattle, or working stock like donkeys or horses. One of my friends in Kenya keeps a deep cement fishpond in the front corner of his yard. It is situated where rain in their neighborhood runs down the dirt road next to their house, and he made a little channel that diverts it into his fishpond. He keeps a species of catfish in it that is common to Lake Victoria close by. I pulled one out with a fishing line the last time I was there, and they cooked it for dinner.

- Gather resources.

Here are some kinds of resources people gather on properties they own, depending on their size and location.

- Rainwater collected in barrels or a cistern or diverted to gardens and fruit trees.
- Water from a well, river, or pond.
- Wood for fires, cooking, and building materials.
- Rocks and gravel for building materials.
- Sand for making cement.
- Mud for making mud huts.
- Mud and straw for making adobe bricks.
- Clay for making bricks or pottery.
- Sunlight to power solar panels.
- Wind to drive windmills for water or electric wind generators.
- Game animals or fish from rivers, lakes, or ponds for food.
- Oil and gas from a well or the royalties.
- Mining minerals or leasing part of your property for mining.

- Business.

I already mentioned working from home, but here my focus is doing other business activities. You might be able to craft products from your home to take to market. You might be able to build a workshop where several people come to create products. You might ship products from your home. You might be able to have a metal fabrication shop or a shoemaking or dressmaking shop at your house. You might be able to open a little produce stand, a convenience store, a restaurant, or a food kiosk on the front of your property along the road. Many of the great businesses of the world started in people's kitchens, living rooms, bedrooms, and garages.

My friend Laura from Rustin, Louisiana, built a thriving interior decorating business. She converted one of the large rooms of her home into a workspace for herself and her employees. It is where they show customers materials and sew and produce drapes, curtains, and furniture covers. She just opened a new commercial property for her business to accommodate their growth. It's a great business, and she started it in their home.

- Rent or lodging.

Another potential value is to rent space on your property for lodging or storage. Many people worldwide rent out extra bedrooms or other spaces for people who need them. Another option is to rent out your whole property and use the income to buy another property.

- Improvements.

I always buy a property based on its future value. The three major factors determining its future value are location, the quality of the buildings and improvements, and the potential for making more improvements while we own it. When I own a property, I keep looking for improvements that we can make that will pay us back with greater use of the property now and greater value when we eventually sell it. Common kinds of improvements are remodeling rooms, adding better fixtures and features, adding on to the building with new rooms or sections, adding detached buildings like a detached garage or shop or shed, and outdoor improvements like landscaping, driveways, patios, pools, wells, driveways, and fencing.

If you don't own it, you can improve it for your temporary use, but that's all. The landlord will get the added value you created when they re-rent or sell it.

- Appreciation.

Of course, one of the great magical characteristics of property is appreciation. Money depreciates due to inflation, but property appreciates. Everywhere around the world where I teach, I ask these questions. First, I take a common amount of their currency and ask, "How much bread could you buy with this amount ten years ago?" They answer with a large amount. Then I ask, "How much bread can you buy with this amount today?" Their answer is a much smaller amount. Then I ask, "Think of a piece of property you wish you had been able to buy ten years ago. What would it have cost then?" They answer. Then I ask, "How much would it cost today?" They always answer with a much higher cost.

That's the magic of property. While money is decreasing in value, property is increasing in value. Think of it as one arrow on a graph going upwards to the right —the value of property - and another arrow going downward to the right – that is the value of money. They are going in opposite directions. It is a simple picture that tells us a powerful truth. We should take as much money as we can and buy as much good property as we can as fast as we can to preserve and create value.

• Loan collateral.

Equity is the value of your property minus any outstanding debt you owe. It is the amount you would make if you sold the home and paid off the debt. If you don't owe any debt, your equity is 100% of the property's value.

Two things happen simultaneously if you are paying for a loan on the property. You are paying the loan balance down with each payment, and your property is probably appreciating. That means you gain more equity in two ways: from your loan payments and the property's appreciation.

Your equity can be used to gain a loan to buy another property, make another investment, or start a business. The lender will place a lien on your property, which means that if you default on the loan, the lender can sell your property to get their money back. So, there is a risk. But it is how many people buy income properties or start businesses.

- Passive income.

    Income from property is considered passive because it is "work-ing" nonstop without your active labor to create value for you. If you have one or more properties that you rent, there is some active work you must do. You must buy it, possibly clean it and fix it up, advertise it, screen potential renters, collect rent, make repairs, and possibly evict renters who do not pay. Or you can hire a property manager who does most of this work for you for a percentage of the rent. Or you can invest in a real estate fund, and it is completely passive. There are different degrees of true "passivity" for you, but the point is that property itself "works" 24/7 to create value. Most businesses don't even do that.

I listed fourteen ways property can create value and much of it simultaneously. That's what makes property so unique and valuable. In contrast, think about money, a stock market investment, or even gold or silver. Can you live on it? Can you do business on it? Can you grow food on it? Can you store your things on it? Can you rent it to others to do these things? No, you can't. These other investments are single-value creators at any given time. That doesn't mean you shouldn't have these other investments, but you should own the best property as soon as possible.

SEVEN IMPLICATIONS OF WEALTH ENGINE #2 OWN

Since property preserves value by transforming money into capital, and capital is the engine of escaping poverty, here are seven implications.

1. Property ownership is the bridge from poverty to prosperity.

If you don't own property, you don't have the best place to put your money to preserve and grow it. That means you will probably keep spending and losing your money. No matter your income, you will not build wealth because it constantly disappears. Your economic life is one bucket, your labor, with a hole in it.

I met with a man yesterday who works in one of the poverty spaces in Asia. He said of the people that he works with, "They don't think about saving money. It's just not in their thought process." They don't even know there is an economic bucket without holes, and they certainly aren't saving any money to get that bucket by buying property.

2. The property we own is the foundation of our wealth creation.

Your creation of value, your work, is the foundation of your income. Your property is the foundation of your wealth.

Income is money coming in, and wealth is money that remains and grows.

3. Socialism and charity fail to solve poverty because they are schemes of shared property but not private property ownership.

Socialism, by definition, rejects private ownership of property and puts it in the hands of the state. This enriches the state and those who politicize their way to the heights of the state apparatus, but it impoverishes everyone else, leaving them with no place to grow wealth.

Charity, by giving away free stuff, creates a false perception for the recipients. It gives the recipients the false idea that they do not need to create income and buy property to create wealth because charities will keep money and things coming to them. But it is a gilded cage of bondage to the charity master.

4. Public policy and infrastructures must support property rights and property ownership.

We will explain these more in Chapter Fifteen: Solve Poverty.

5. Every organization working in the poverty space should be empowering the poor to become property owners.

Poverty space organizations should work to put policies and infrastructures in place that promote and protect property ownership. And they should be teaching and facilitating the poor to become property owners.

I am not saying just to give people property or put them in loans they can't afford. I am saying that the poor should be helped to step upward economically by creating greater value to earn more income, saving money toward buying a property, and then getting into their first property, even if it is very modest. They need to get an economic foot-hold in a property that provides good value for them. Then, they can stair-step upward with better property as their incomes and wealth grow.

6. Wealth Engines #1 CREATE and #2 OWN create a virtuous relationship between income and wealth creation.

Creating value is an economically virtuous *action*. It creates new money.

Creating value and buying property is an economically virtuous *relationship*.

CREATE produces income. OWN produces wealth.

7. To flourish, we must create the best value and own the best property as soon as we can.

Time is of the essence because the sooner you own a property, the sooner you quit losing money on rent, and the sooner your property builds equity and appreciated wealth.

I started this chapter with the odd story of our childhood caliche wars. The point was not the caliche wars as much as it was the fact that I grew up in a culture where owning our homes was the norm, where our church's owning their properties was the norm, and where owning business properties was the norm. If we wanted to build on them, sell them, or have caliche wars on them, we could. We were free to do so. And we were growing wealth through that property ownership. We were transforming the money we created through our work into capital with roots. The ministry properties we owned and developed created millions of dollars of value and tens of thousands of souls' worth of impact. The business properties created millions of dollars of wealth. And our peoples' homes and properties created hundreds of millions of dollars of wealth.

In chapter ten, I will teach ten ways to own the best property you can.

Before that, let's look at the *"You Should Rent" Fallacy*. It is a common error that prevents many from escaping poverty and building wealth.

Chapter Nine
The You-Should-Rent Fallacy

MOST PEOPLE RENT BECAUSE THEY have to. They can't afford to buy property, they don't know they should, they don't know how, or the policies and infrastructures that promote property ownership don't exist where they live. You should buy unless one of the following situations applies to you.

First, if you just can't put enough money together for the downpayment and the monthly payments or one big payment.

Second, if you have acquired enough wealth that you don't want to create more for your life, your heirs, or the causes you support, then you have a case for the simplicity of renting. However, the few people I know in this situation can't stand the thought of not leveraging where they live as an investment. They hate not putting their money to work.

Third, if you do not plan to live in a location for more than three to five years, you have a case to rent rather than buy a place to live. Owning a home takes three to five years for the economic benefits to outweigh the lower costs and responsibilities of renting. It only takes about three years in a hot property market where homes appreciate at 5 to 10 percent per year or more. In an average market where homes appreciate about 3 to 5 percent per year, it takes about five years.

We moved to the Dallas area four years ago. We bought it with equity from our previous house plus our ability to make payments on a loan. We bought the best house we could within our budget, and it was a hot market. I have discovered that when we move to a new place, it takes us about three years to figure out where we would prefer to live. So, around the three-year mark, we started looking for a house of similar value to ours, but in another location that we preferred and with some features we preferred. When we sold that first Dallas house, we were pleasantly surprised at how much more it sold for than what we paid three and a half years earlier. That short-term home ownership was well worth it because it was a hot market.

We made these decisions about buying versus renting because we understand the "bucketology" of it. Here is the bucketology illustration and explanation.

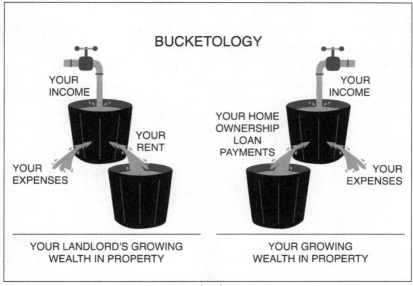

Bucketology

Everyone has at least one economic bucket. It is your income and expenses bucket. Your income fills your bucket with money, and your expenses are a hole in your bucket that drains it out.

Some people have a magic bucket that does not have a hole in it. That bucket is a property they own or are buying with a loan, called a mortgage.

If you are renting, your rent is paying your landlord's mortgage in his or her magic bucket. You are building their wealth.

If you are buying your property with a mortgage, your mortgage payment is growing your wealth.

As a rule, the poor are renters, and the rich are property owners and landlords. This is why the rich get richer and the poor do not. The rich have a second bucket without holes, but the poor do not. This means that you need to buy the best property you can as soon as you can to stop losing money and start building some wealth.

Still, some will advocate for you to continue as a renter. The usual reasons cited for the you-should-rent fallacy are these:

- No maintenance or repair costs or hassles. Your landlord takes care of them.
- Access to amenities at your rental apartment or neighborhood.
- No real estate taxes. Your landlord pays them.
- No property insurance. You may choose a cheaper renter's insurance, but your landlord pays for the property insurance.
- No downpayment, just a cheaper first and last month's rent to get in.
- Less responsibility and hassle.
- More flexibility to move when you want.
- Fewer concerns over the possibility of decreasing property value.
- Rent is usually lower than a house payment.
- Lower utilities costs.

These may be somewhat true, but they still overlook the biggest truth. Renting is an economic bucket with a hole in it, and it misses the opportunity to grow wealth with property.

I say these points are somewhat true because you pay for amenities, insurance, taxes, and repairs when you rent. You pay for them through your rent. Landlords don't pay for these things out of the goodness of their hearts. They must make a profit, or they will go out of business. That means they pay for them with your rent. Most rental properties are less desirable in location, size, useability, security, peace, and quiet than places you would buy. By the way, the poorer places in the world are usually the noisiest. People pay a premium for peace and quiet. So, your rent is usually less than a loan payment for a home because it is a less desirable place to live. You are getting what you pay for.

So, should you pay less for just one bucket with a hole or more for a second bucket without a hole? What kind of bucket would you get if you had to haul water for a mile? One with a hole or one without a hole? It's the same decision but with much bigger consequences.

The same applies to a property for a business, ministry, nonprofit organization, or anything else. If you rent or lease, you leak money and build your landlord's wealth. If you buy it, your second bucket grows your organization's wealth.

Do these two things to move forward in the Spirit of Creation and Wealth Engines #1 and #2. First, create the best value you can. Second, own the best property you can.

Of course, moving from renting to owning is a big leap for most people. So how do you do it? In the next chapter, I will teach you ten ways to own the best property you can.

Let's get that second magic bucket without holes!

Chapter Ten
Ten Ways to Own the Best Property You Can

PASTOR BARNABAS LIVES IN NORTHWEST Tanzania and has practiced CREATE, OWN, and GROW. He pastors a village church, farms some land, and trains for our organization, PPI. He creates value and receives income from each of these works. He owns his home and farming plots; his church owns land with a humble mud hut church building.

I loved the opportunity to train at his village church, The First Baptist Church of Rorya, Tanzania. The people live simple lives, but they are smart. All I had to illustrate the three wealth engines of CREATE, OWN, and GROW were three big pieces of butcher paper and some markers. We drew it up and taught it through two levels of interpreters, from English to Swahili to their local tribal language. And they were fired up after two days of training. Pastor Barnabas had seen how his friend, George Kienga, in Kenya, practiced it. The people had seen how Pastor Barnabas was practicing it. They heard the biblical and economic explanations of it, they heard and saw the illustrations we gave, and they heard several of our Kenyan team members describe how they were practicing it and seeing it done.

Recently, Pastor Barnabas seized a chance to raise his wealth engines to new levels. He got 125 acres of farmland through a program with the Tanzanian government, where he can pay a relatively low amount for the land for the opportunity to farm it for five years. If he farms it for five years, the government will give him the deed to the property. He has workers clearing the field now of trees, and they will be plowing and planting soon. He will also start a second church close to that land. He is also working to extend his training work for PPI across Tanzania and other African countries. As I write this, he is en route to the Democratic Republic of the Congo to train multiple churches in multiple cities in the Spirit of Creation.

Pastor Barnabas works among some of the poorest people in Africa and is an example of how to rise out of poverty through the Spirit of Creation. His efforts to acquire this large piece of farmland will change his family's destiny for generations. It will give him a new source of agri-business income and a large second bucket without holes. He is getting his bucketology working for him.

To help you get your bucketology working, here are ten ways to own the best property you can.

TEN WAYS TO OWN THE BEST PROPERTY YOU CAN

1. Think of yourself as a property owner.

If your family does not have a history of owning property, or if you believe that you will probably not become a property owner, you must start by changing how you think about yourself. Your first act toward becoming a property owner is not about property. It is about yourself. We all have stories about ourselves that we repeat in our minds. Often, they are limiting beliefs that keep us from doing things we could and should do. We have to change those limiting beliefs to do bigger things.

You may have thought you are not good, smart, or rich enough to own property. You may have thought that property owners belong to a higher class of people than you, so it will be out of your reach. The most important limiting factor that will keep you from owning property is the limitations of your mind. You have to change your story with a new story that says these things:

- I am a child of God created in the image of God.
- God created me to create value and make a good living, and I will.
- God placed me on the material earth where he gives his people the right to own property for their security and prosperity, so I will.
- I will take these ten steps to own property, even if it takes my whole life, and then I will pass the legacy of property ownership down to my children.

The last phrase of this new story is important because as you gain the Spirit of Creation and practice the Three Biblical Wealth Engines, you are creating a legacy of new thinking, action, and results for your family's future. Your children and grandchildren will live in the shadow of the empowerment legacy you create or neglect.

2. Think of property ownership as your path to prosperity.

In the last two chapters, we have made the case that owning property is one of your key paths to prosperity. However, you will still hear voices that will tell you differently.

Some of those voices may come from your head. If they do, reread these last three chapters to reset your mind on the truth.

Some of those voices will come from others. They may come from family members or friends. If they do, politely decide not to follow their advice.

Some of those voices will come from "experts" about finances. Don't listen to them, either. They may be able to make a case that you will save money in the short term, but you will be losing money and wealth in the long run. You must act for the long run because you need to prepare for your later years when you will have less energy and capacity to create value to make money, and you need to create a legacy of wealth that will continue for your children and grandchildren. To live for our future and the futures of our children and succeeding generations is a characteristic of the Christian worldview because we are working to grow the kingdom of God on this earth for as long as it lasts and then to be part of Christ's eternal kingdom in the New Heaven and New Earth (Revelation 21).

Some of the voices will come from socialist globalists like Danish politician Ida Auken, who wrote an essay for the World Economic Forum stating that in the future, "You will own nothing, and be happy,"[23] and mega-wealth management firms that are reported to have schemes to buy every private residence.[24] Property will always belong to someone, and those with it have the power. If the government or the government in partnership with mega-corporations owns all property, it has all the power, and there is no room for personal freedom. It is, then, by definition, a tyranny. Individual property ownership is a God-given right because it is a necessary means by which we have freedom, security, and prosperity.

Property ownership is essential to your economic well-being, your political freedom, and your religious freedom. Every voice that tells you it is unimportant does not understand one or all of these truths or is lying to you for bad reasons. Get your head straight on this truth.

3. Set your goal and plan to own property.

A goal is a *what* by *when*, and a plan is a set of steps to get there. A goal without a plan and the execution of that plan is just a wish. So, set your goal and plan to own property.

Set the date by when you want to and think you could own property. It may be one, two, five, ten, or twenty years later. But set that date, write it down, and place that written goal where you can see it often. Your goal may be to own a property by a certain age.

Then, write out the steps you will take to own property. They may look like this:

- Save a set amount of money for a downpayment.
- Be looking for potential properties to buy.
- Find two or three properties that are options to buy.
- Look for the three Ds to get the best deals in buying property: Death, Disease, or Divorce. Often, when people go through these crisis events, they or their families are ready to sell their properties, often at lower prices than before. It is not taking advantage of their misfortune if you negotiate with them in good faith. It helps them get the sale they want so they can move on to other things in their lives. I have purchased three homes we have lived in that were available for sale at lower-than-usual prices because of death or divorce. I have purchased eight properties that we have used as rental income, and we got a below-normal price because of death or divorce. In all cases, they were happy to make the sale, get their money, get rid of having to manage those properties and move on.
- Negotiate with the owners to buy their properties with payments to them or with payments on a loan that you get from a third party, like a bank, mortgage company, SACCO (Saving and Credit Co-Operative Society in Africa), or loan company.
- Buy the property.

4. Pay off your debt.

If you have consumer debt, pay it off. Consumer debt is debt on something that is now gone, like a vacation or a wedding, or something that is losing money, like a car, boat, or recreational vehicle. It is important to pay it off so you can start saving money to buy property to grow wealth,

If you have credit card debt, pay it off as quickly as you can.

The snowball method is one of the best strategies for paying off consumer debt. First, pay as much as you can on your smallest debt to pay it off as quickly as you can. Getting it paid off has a psychological benefit and a financial benefit. You feel great for paying it off, and it encourages you to keep going. You also have more money now to pay off the next highest debt with as much extra money as you can as fast as you can. So, you keep doing this. The whole thing snowballs or grows with momentum as you pay off each debt.

5. Save money to buy property.

Saving money requires three things. First, you must have a goal bigger than your desire to spend money on personal consumer goods. Second, you must create a budget to plan what you will spend and save. Third, you must develop thrifty habits, where you don't spend when you don't need to.

Your goal may be to own property. Your bigger goal may be to help your children get an education, to be able to live comfortably in retirement, to start a business, or to fund your calling or a dream you have. That goal must always be clear, compelling, and in front of you.

Your budget, or spending plan, must be reasonable and doable. Here are the steps to creating it and following it:

- Start with your expected income for the week or month.
- List your have-to expenses like tithe, rent, payments, utilities, etc..
- Subtract the total of your have-to expenses from your total income, giving you your flexible spending.
- Be as frugal as you can be with your flexible spending. Subtract that from the running total.
- What's left is what you can save.
- Set those savings aside in a place that is hard to touch.

The next step is to establish some habits of thrift. Thrift means not spending on things that you don't need to. One old saying of thriftiness is, "Use it, reuse it, fix it, use it again, and use it up." Often, we would like to buy something new because it makes us feel better, but we don't need it. We need to find ways of feeling good about being thrifty.

Two examples of thrifty successful people are Sam Walton, the founder of Walmart, and Warren Buffet, the world-famous investing guru. They both live in modest houses that have been paid off for many years, and they drive old trucks or cars that have been long paid off instead of spending their money on lavish houses, cars, and yachts. They found joy in thrift and built great wealth. Warren Buffet is never seen at expensive entertainment venues like professional football games or concerts. He does meet with friends one night a week to play bridge.

My parents and my wife's parents were examples of thrifty living. My dad and my father-in-law usually fixed most things that broke themselves. They would never pay someone else to do it if they could do it themselves. One picture I will never forget is my father-in-law's cardboard box that he used for a traveling toolbox. He co-owned a small airplane, and his part of the ownership group was to do the mechanical maintenance on it. I watched him load up the tools he would need many times in an old ratty cardboard box to take to the airport to work on his airplane. Early on, I thought it was kind of crazy because he could easily afford a nice new toolbox. But then it inspired me because he could afford to be a co-owner and pilot of an airplane, but he also found ways where he didn't need to spend money, and he didn't care what anyone thought about him. His financial goals were more important than what others thought.

My wife and I live in a nice house and have a nice life. But from the time we were married until now, one of our hobbies has been buying some of the things we need at thrift stores. We have had many date nights or afternoons, including getting lunch or dinner and going to a thrift store. In my early days, my suits and dress clothes were from thrift stores. They looked great, but I bought them used. My wife's latest great find at a thrift store was a bread maker in great shape. She recently became a sourdough bread maker and uses the bread machine for some dessert bread. It was a fraction of the cost of a new one. We both have fun finding ways to be thrifty and not spending what we don't need to. It is one of the things that has allowed us to save money, and we put it into property to grow our wealth.

6. Look for a good property to buy.

I always buy a property for its future value. I see its value in five, ten, or twenty years and compare it to the cost of buying and improving it. The properties with the best future value compared to those expenses are good to buy. I also consider the usefulness of the property and its possible income.

Here are some things that make a property a good buy:

- It is in a good location. As is often said, the three most important things about a property's value are its location, location, location.
- It is offered at a good price for the value of the property.
- You can afford the down payment, regular payments, utilities, taxes, and insurance.
- You can make good use of it.
- It can be a home for you.
- You can rent part or all of it out to tenants.
- It will appreciate at a good rate. The surrounding area is improving in value.
- You can improve it.
- You can do some business on it.
- It is in the path of growth, development, or re-development.
- It has resources like water, wood, minerals, animals, or places to grow crops or raise livestock.

7. Buy your first property.

Buying your first property can be scary. After you buy it, you may feel buyer's remorse for a while because it is a big commitment. But take heart. If you checked off most of the things you need to buy a good property, you will be okay. If you don't like owning it in a year or so, sell it.

But at some point, you need to jump in and make a property purchase.

When I am training in the developing world in high-poverty communities, I often say that if all you can afford is a very small piece of property big enough for you to put up the most modest livable shack, plant a small garden, and raise a few chickens, then buy it. Buy it and fix it up as you can. Then, in a year or two, rent it out for more than what it costs you in payments and other costs, or sell it for more than you paid. Either way, it can give you a beginning in property ownership to move up and buy better property next time. But you must jump in somewhere to get the value of owning property that increases in value.

8. Maintain and improve your property.

To maximize the value of your property and your enjoyment of it, maintain it and improve it. Keep it clean, repaired, and updated. Make improvements worth the cost for your added enjoyment, and that has a good chance of paying you back when you sell it.

Here are some possible improvements:

- Landscaping.
- Fencing and a gate.
- Gardens.
- Livestock pens or corrals.
- Barns.
- Remodeling the kitchen or a bathroom.
- Painting the interior or exterior of your house.
- Adding parking areas.
- Adding covered parking or garage space.
- Building an addition onto your house.

My life has felt like a long property development project with the houses we have owned. We have remodeled and expanded almost every house we have owned. I envision improving and expanding the house and property where we live now. I am working on the first of those improvements: remodeling an attached apartment. Sweat equity made our homes more enjoyable places to live and more valuable when we sold them. Improving a property and its value is one of the joys of owning it for me.

9. Consider selling your property to buy a better one.

Several things happen as you make the payments on your house over time. First, you gain more home equity from paying down your loan.

Equity is the value of your house minus what you owe. So, if your house is worth $100,000 and you owe $60,000, your equity is $40,000. It is the amount you will get if you sell it. Second, the value of your house is probably appreciating or growing because property tends to increase in value over time. So, your home may be worth $110,000 because of appreciation. If you owe $60,000 in this case, your equity would be $50,000. Third, if you made some improvements to your home, it might be worth $120,000, including the appreciation. If you owed $60,000 in this case, your equity would be $60,000.

If you sold your house, you would have $60,000 plus any other savings to buy a new house. The $60,000 alone would be a 20% down payment on a home that costs $300,000. That would work if you could afford the payments on the remaining loan of $240,000. At any rate, this example shows how, over time, owning a property grows your wealth so you can buy a better property later.

When you sell a house to take advantage of your equity to buy a more valuable house, you are growing your wealth engine because the more valuable house grows more in value and equity over time. It is a bigger engine that creates more wealth. This is why we say you should own the best property you can. Again, we don't mean buying more than you can afford, but buy the best property you can afford because it will grow your wealth the most.

10. Invest your equity.

You can use your equity to start or expand a business. If you have a proven business concept and need money to start it, you can do what many other business owners have done: Get a loan against your home equity to fund it. Since you are betting your house, you better have a great business concept and a commitment to making it work. If you do, this is an option to leverage your wealth in your home to multiply value through a business.

Another option is to buy an investment property. You could use your equity to purchase or make the down payment on a property you rent to a tenant. The rental income would need to be more than your property loan payments and other costs of owning it. You might not make much on the rental income, but the real benefit is that your tenant would be making your loan payment on the property. You would get the value of your equity growth and the appreciation of the property. So, it usually takes five years or more to get the best value out of rental properties.

Another option is to buy property for your business. Your business may be doing well, and between your home equity and your business income, you could buy a property for your business. You would be paying your home equity loan back to pay off the property while you gain several benefits. Your business would be in a property you own and can improve for greater value. You would never face the problem of your landlord raising your rent, canceling your lease, or selling the property. You would gain equity and appreciation in your business property just like you do in your home. It's surprising how many people own their homes but don't try to buy rather than lease a property for their business. They take the short-term gain of a tax break for the business costs of rent but miss the long-term gain of growing wealth through their business property.

Those who buy their business properties have another asset that has grown that they can sell or transfer to the future owners of their business. Or they can keep the property and rent it back to the new owner for an income stream. Ray Kroc, the founder of the McDonald's hamburger restaurants, is famous for saying, "We are not in the hamburger business. We are in the real estate business."[25] You will notice that McDonald's restaurants tend to be on some of the most valuable commercial properties. Ray Kroc realized that the real long-term and greater wealth was in real estate, not hamburgers. He saw hamburgers as the way to buy real estate. If you own a business, whatever your business does could help you buy property, and your home equity could help you make that purchase.

Your home equity is a source of built-up wealth that you can put to work with a home equity loan to pay for an investment worth more than your interest and principal payments. The investment must be wise; if it is, it can be well worth it.

Here, again, are the Ten Ways to Own the Best Property You Can.

1. **Think of Yourself as a Property Owner.**
2. **Think of Property Ownership as Your Way to Prosperity.**
3. **Set Your Goal and Plan to Own Property.**
4. **Pay Off Your Debt.**
5. **Save Money to Buy Property.**

6. Look for a Good Property to Buy.
7. Buy Your First Property.
8. Maintain and Improve Your Property.
9. Consider Selling Your Property to Buy a Better One.
10. Invest Your Equity.

Combined with Biblical Wealth Engine #1 CREATE, Wealth Engine #2 OWN forms a process of income and wealth creation. Creating value creates income. That income can be used to own property. The wealth from that property ownership can create more opportunities to create more value. The added income can help you buy more or better property. CREATE and OWN form a virtuous relationship to create income and wealth.

Next, we will move to the Biblical Wealth Engine #3 GROW. When all three engines are at work in your life, they create a virtuous *cycle* of income and wealth creation, not just a process. Here, again, is the diagram of that cycle.

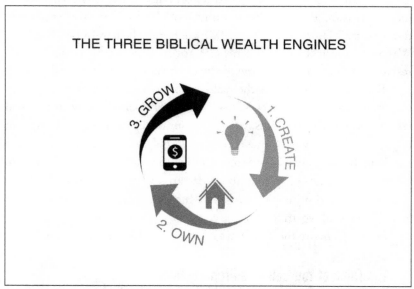

THE THREE BIBLICAL WEALTH ENGINES

The Three Biblical Wealth Engines

Now let's learn Wealth Engine #3 GROW.

Chapter Eleven
Wealth Engine #3 GROW:
Business Multiplies Value

AS A BOY IN WESTERN Kenya at the age of fifteen, John Bosco lost his parents. That left him homeless with three siblings to care for. They lived on and off the streets as their income changed with John's periodic jobs as a domestic or farm worker.

Then John attended a training course on the Spirit of Creation at George Kienga's Annual Biblical Economic Empowerment Conference, which he leads each August outside of the town of Awendo in Migori County. George has become a legend of economic empowerment with his farm businesses, award-winning private school, and medical clinic. He teaches the Spirit of Creation in his school, to his neighboring farmers, and young people at his annual conference.

It opened John Bosco's eyes to new ways of thinking and acting about life, work, money, faith, and God. He started creating new value where he was and with what he had. He began collecting seeds and cuttings from trees in his area and planting them in discarded plastic containers. As they sprouted and stabilized, he would sell them on the busy streets of Awendo beside the hundreds of other outdoor vendors. His sales began to pick up, and he hired a few students to help him. His sales continued to rise, and he hired a few more students to help him gather seeds and cuttings, plant them, and sell them.

Then he got his big break. The Migori County government contracted him to plant trees in their environmental development program. He ramped up his operation and hired fifty students. The business grew to selling 200 seedling trees a day. John bought three parcels of land and built a home for himself and his siblings. He finished his education and is paying for his siblings to finish theirs.

Like his mentor, George Kienga, John is a committed Christian who supports his church and other ministries. He is a Christian leader in business and life. John is now a regular speaker at George Kienga's annual training conference. He is part of a movement of economically empowered African Christians changing Africa with the Spirit of Creation.

John learned to apply the Three Biblical Wealth Engines of CREATE, OWN, and GROW. All three are important in different ways, but the one that generates the most money is the last one, GROW. It is business. Business is the biggest economic engine of all, funding everything that matters. It changed John Bosco's life, and it can change yours.

Let's start with the economic principle that explains why. The principle of Wealth Engine #3 GROW is closely tied to the principle of Wealth Engine #1 CREATE. They are the *same action* at *different scales*. CREATE is the addition of new money by creating new value through one's direct labor. It is addition. Wealth Engine #3 GROW is the multiplication of new money by creating new value through multiple factors of creation. It is multiplication.

The statement of the principle of Wealth Engine #3 GROW is this: *Business multiplies value.*

THE ECONOMIC PRINCIPLE OF MULTIPLICATION

The economic principle is that business multiplies value. It differs from one's direct labor in how many factors of creation are put to work. In one's labor, one factor is put to work: one's labor. In business, multiple factors are put to work. That is the defining characteristic of business. Five common factors of creation that can be put to work in a business are people's labor, specialized knowledge, equipment and supplies, property, and money. These multiple factors of creation multiply the products, services, and solutions produced. This is how business multiplies the creation of money.

Addition is good, and you should create as much value and money as you can by creating the best value you can through your work. But multiplication is better, and you should also grow the best business you can to multiply money. Don't worry, we know everyone is not wired to be an entrepreneur, and in Chapter Thirteen, we will give you two other roles you can fill to benefit from the economic power of growing businesses.

Some people are called to work alone to create the best values in the world, and that's just fine. But, in the economy, far more money is created by working together in businesses. They are harnessing the power of multiple factors of creation being put to work and the specialized capabilities of different people to create multiplied and even exponential value together. One person can write a beautiful symphony, but it takes hundreds of people to produce an amazing evening of an orchestra playing that symphony in a beautiful indoor or outdoor theater. It takes musicians, musical instrument makers and sellers, conductors, symphony managers, architects, builders, event producers and managers, and many others. It also takes a team of many people to create an In-N-Out Burger system of restaurants that feeds hundreds of thousands of people and creates hundreds of millions of dollars.

This is why business is the most powerful engine of wealth creation for nations, communities, families, and individuals. It multiplies wealth because it puts multiple factors of wealth creation to work.

In addition to the economic truth, we see this reflected in biblical principles.

THE BIBLICAL AND HISTORIC CHRISTIAN CASE FOR BUSINESS

The Bible, Jewish culture, and Christian culture are pro-business. This value is rooted in the earliest stories in the Bible.

The business culture of the Bible is established in the beginning, in Genesis.

First, God creates the massive value of the universe and the earth, and then he places his image bearers endowed with creative abilities into that environment. And God blessed them with the job of using their God-given abilities to create new value to make it better.

Then God placed the first two people as a team into a perfect environment to create even more value together as they tended the garden, related to God, and related to each other.

After the fall of man into sin and the murder of Abel by his brother Cain, the Bible describes the division of industries in the human population as agriculture, metal fabrication, and the arts in Genesis 4:19-22.

So, we see people making their living and practicing their gifts in trades and businesses.

The next major character in the Bible is Noah. According to Michael Eisenberg, the author of *The Tree of Life and Prosperity: 21st Century Business Principles from the Book of Genesis*, Noah was quite the entrepreneur. Not only did he build the ark that saved humanity from extinction, but he was also the first to plant a vineyard to produce wine, and he invented the plow.[26]

Genesis 5:29 says, "He [Noah's father Lamech] named him Noah and said, 'He will comfort us in the labor and painful toil of our hands caused by the ground the Lord has cursed." The Jewish scholars of the Midrash concluded that this statement and Noah being called a "man of the soil" in Genesis 9:20 was evidence that Noah was the inventor of the plow. It is how he gave relief to the people from the hard labor of breaking up the soil with their hands or sticks.

Eisenberg concludes that Noah's invention created cultural wealth. It not only enriched Noah, but it enriched all who began to use plows. It increased their food productivity and reduced the labor required for it. He also believes that the added leisure it brought to the ancient world was part of the reason that people descended into so much evil that God decided to destroy the world with the flood. He also believes that Noah's invention and plow manufacturing and sales financed his massive project of building the ark. He was the original John Deere farm implement producer, and that business financed his ark project. Inventing a new kind of steel plow for the American prairie soil in 1837 was how John Deere got his start.[27]

It makes sense that this is how Noah financed the ark because its dimensions show that it was a massive project that would require massive resources and labor. And Noah was a man of the soil, not a man of carpentry. He probably had to hire many carpenters. People mocked Noah for building the ark, but one can always find people to work for decent pay, no matter the project.

Simply put, Noah could not have done what he did in building the ark if he did not have the resources to build it that came from business. These include multiple people's labor, specialized knowledge in carpentry, tools, timber, property to build it on, and money to pay the laborers. Noah saved humanity not only through faith but also through business.

Then, when God called a man to go to the Promised Land by faith and to become the father of God's people by faith, he didn't choose a priest, an artist, or a teacher. He chose a businessman. Abraham was in the livestock business, and you better believe it was a business. Genesis 12:5 says that Abraham set out from Haran: "He took his wife Sarai, his nephew Lot, all the possessions they had accumulated and the people he acquired in Haran…" It makes sense that Abraham was already in the livestock business because most people received their trades from their families. Once they arrived in Canaan, they fled to Egypt because of a famine. While there, it says, "…Abram acquired sheep, cattle, male and female donkeys, menservants and maidservants, and camels" (Genesis 12:16). Then Genesis 13:2 says, "Abram had become very wealthy in livestock and in silver and gold."

Abram acquired these things because that was his business. He knew livestock, and he pursued growing his herds. God blessed him, but he also worked on growing his business.

The story moves to the conflict between Abram's and Lot's herdsmen, who had such large herds that the land they were trying to use was not big enough for them. This is a classic Western movie motif. So, they separated. Notice that neither Abram nor Lot were in the fields tending the herds. They had hired people for that. They ran their businesses.

In Genesis 14, Lot and his people and herds are abducted by four warlords, and Abram goes after them. Genesis 14:14 says, "When Abram heard that his relative had been taken captive, he called out 318 trained men born in his household and went in pursuit as far as Dan." It goes on to say that Abram routed them and recovered Lot, his people, his possessions, and the spoils of the battle.

From where did these 318 trained fighting men come? They were "born in his household," either literally or figuratively. They were part of the traveling village of men, women, and children that made up Abraham's economy of a vast livestock business. Imagine if the average fighting-age man had at least one wife, if not several, and at least three children, if not more. These men and their families would have made up a nomadic community of 1,590 people connected to Abram Livestock, Inc. That's a big business operation.

Abraham's son, Isaac, also became rich in the agriculture business. Genesis 26:13-14 says, "Isaac planted crops in the land and the same year reaped a hundredfold because the Lord blessed him. The man became rich and grew until he became very wealthy. He had so many flocks and herds and servants that the Philistines envied him."

Isaac's son, Jacob, also built his flocks and herds while he worked in the service of his father-in-law, Laban. When he returned to Canaan to reunite with his brother Esau, the Bible describes them both as wealthy with flocks, herds, and servants.

Jacob (also called Israel) had twelve sons who became the heads of the twelve tribes of Israel. The older brothers captured their younger brother Joseph because they were jealous of him, and they sold him to Midianite traders who sold him on the auction block in Egypt. That began the greatest rags-to-riches story ever told.

Joseph rose from slavery through multiple setbacks and, with God's blessings, became the second in command of the Pharoah in Egypt. He became the minister of the economy and oversaw the plan God had given him to prepare Egypt to survive a historic famine. Through God's guidance and sound business acumen, Joseph saved his family, which saved the nation of Israel. He also saved many Egyptians and others who came to buy food there (Genesis 37-50). He grew the Pharoah's wealth in livestock, money, and land acquisitions (Genesis 47:13-20). He saved all of these through shrewd business decisions. That ends the book of Genesis.

The next major figure is Moses in Exodus. Under Moses, God gave the Law of Moses, which served as the constitution for the new nation of Israel, which they received before possessing the Promised Land. The Law of Moses created the policies that supported the creation of wealth, property ownership, and business growth. It provided policies such as the rule of law (Leviticus 19:15), honesty in financial transactions (Leviticus 19:36), and property rights (Exodus 20:15 & Deuteronomy 19:14). It was a pro-business constitution.

Genesis is the foundational book of the Bible, establishing a biblical worldview about life, God, people, human purpose, human value, human nature, right and wrong, work, and money. The next is the Law of Moses in Exodus, Leviticus, Numbers, and Deuteronomy. Both establish the Spirit of Creation as the biblical economic ethos, with business being a key part.

The next major body of truth comes from the teachings of Jesus. Rev. Dr. Robert Sirico, the founder of the Acton Institute, theologian, and economist, has written *The Economics of the Parables*. He writes about the economic assumptions and principles in thirteen of the great parables of Jesus. If I may paraphrase the many statements he makes about the economics of Jesus' parables, it would be that the Spirit of Creation, established in the Old Testament, and the righteousness of business done properly is assumed and supported by Jesus in these great teaching stories.

The premiere parable of this type is the parable of the talents in Matthew 25, where three servants are given money by their master to invest in some business venture. The ones who invested well in business were commended and rewarded. The one who buried the money for safekeeping was condemned and judged as lazy and wicked. This parable uses business truths to make a point about spiritual truths. In using this parable, Jesus affirms both truths. We must invest the talents God gives us in service of his kingdom and invest our resources well on this earth to create more. And that is done through business.

The final biblical body of revelation is the New Testament epistles. The Apostle Paul, under the inspiration of the Holy Spirit, wrote most of them. Paul's economic teaching is most clearly seen in the I & II Thessalonians. According to the commentary on them by Gene L. Greene, Paul addressed economic abuses by the Thessalonians, who were part of the culture of Thessalonica. Thessalonica was a Roman government town. It garrisoned a large contingent of Roman soldiers and had many influential Roman families who ran businesses with concessions granted by Rome. It was a town where the system of patrons and clients was in play economically. The patrons were wealthy business-owning families. The clients were the common people who would line up in the morning at their doors to do the favors asked by the patron managers. Some days, they had things to do, and some days, they didn't. Those who were loyal servants of the patrons and did their favors were rewarded with money, protection, and favors. The actions taken by the clients could involve political support or running errands. The patron-client system was reflected in what would become the Sicilian mafia. It was an economy of who knew whom and who did what for whom rather than an economy of creating wealth. It was filled with corruption, from how the families got their concessions from Rome to how the clients worked for the patrons. It was not an employer-employee relationship with clear roles, work, and pay within proper ethics. It was the spirit of connections and corruption rather than the Spirit of Creation. Unfortunately, it characterizes the dynamics of modern political and corporate corruption. This spirit also animates those who rise in power and money in socialism.

To combat this, Paul took no donations from the Thessalonian church but rather worked with his hands at his tentmaking trade to demonstrate how they should do the same rather than being idol "busybodies" (I Thessalonians 5:11-12 & II Thessalonians 3:6-15). It made sense for Paul to be supported in the ministry and concentrate on that higher work. Still, in this case, he denied himself that right to teach the Thessalonians the Spirit of Creation versus the spirit of being a busybody.[28]

The Bible teaches the Spirit of Creation as the foundational economic principle. The three specific principles and practices were creating value, owning property, and growing business. That's why the Jewish culture worldwide is a culture of wealth creation and business. That's why Christianity, when it reaches a critical mass of influence, influences cultures toward the Spirit of Creation, resulting in prosperity and human flourishing. And business is at the heart of that ethic.

Growing business is a Christian ethic. That was the thesis of Max Weber's book, *The Protestant Ethic and the Spirit of Capitalism,* published in Germany in 1904. He claimed that this ethic or ethos or spirit in Protestant Christianity gave rise to the historic economic revolution that brought more people out of the lower class into the middle class in Europe than had ever happened before.[29]

The next big historic economic miracle was the American economy. It was based on the principles of the Declaration of Independence and the American Constitution, infused with the biblical political worldview of freedom and the economic worldview of the Spirit of Creation. The American government and many of the major American institutions are now laden with godlessness and corruption and the spirit of anything but creation. But at its zenith, the American Spirit of Creation that came from its founding principles and its culture of business changed the world. It became the global exporter of the Spirit of Creation. The nations trying to practice the Spirit of Creation and grow businesses are now on the rise.

The biblical and Christian worldview affirms the righteousness and power of business to create the wealth of nations, communities, families, and individuals. As we did for CREATE and OWN, we will give seven implications of these truths about GROW.

THE SEVEN IMPLICATIONS OF WEALTH ENGINE #3 GROW: BUSINESS MULTIPLIES VALUE

1. Business done properly is one of the most righteous things we can do.

Since the essence of business is multiplying value and since it is key to human flourishing and fulfilling our human mission from God, it is one of the most righteous things we can do. To believe this, many must overcome the fallacy that says business is evil. This myth is popular in almost all cultures, including Christian culture. We will address this fallacy in the next chapter.

2. Business is the generator of wealth in a society.

CREATE, OWN, and GROW are the Three Wealth Engines, but the last one, business, is the mega-engine of prosperity. As the culture of business goes, so does the prosperity of the people.

Since business multiplies value by combining multiple factors of value creation, it is the primary birthplace of money in the economy. It funds everything else: the government, the non-profit sector, ministries, all wages, and all new businesses.

3. The community of Christians in every culture should create an ecosystem of wealth

The community of Christians in any community, culture, or world can also be called the Church. Whether it is the Church on the Navajo Reservation in the Southwestern United States, the Church in New York City, or the Church in any part of Africa, among many things it should be, it should be an ecosystem of businesses that create human flourishing.

It is our biblical and historical heritage and calling to bless the world spiritually, socially, and economically through ecosystems of good business.

Chrisitan communities should create ecosystems of business and wealth and shape the broader cultures around them to do the same. Chrisitan communities should save souls, solve poverty, and create human flourishing for as many as possible.

4. Every organization working in the poverty space should empower the poor to grow businesses.

Missions, ministries, nonprofits, and NGOs working in the poverty space should teach the poor the economic wisdom, spiritual righteousness, and social nobility of growing businesses. They should be teaching the knowledge and skills to grow businesses. And they should be creating empowering partnerships to help them create healthy business ecosystems.

5. Socialism and toxic charity fail to solve poverty and create prosperity because they suppress the creation of businesses.

Socialism, by definition, suppresses the freedom of private ownership of business and centralizes its control and direction under the state. It then runs those businesses into eventual destruction by managing them by political rather than business criteria.

Toxic charity is the overuse of charity and the neglect of empowering the poor with the Spirit of Creation. It suppresses the growth of business among the poor in two ways. First, it creates dependence and passivity among the poor by giving them charity without or instead of economic empowerment. Second, toxic charity suppresses the empowerment of the poor to become self-sufficient business owners to maintain the codependency between them and the poor. No one says it that way, but it is what often happens if we are brutally honest. That's one of the theses of the book *Toxic Charity* and the documentary film *Poverty, Inc.*

6. Policies and infrastructures in communities and nations must be pro-business for people to flourish.

Policies are the laws and official procedures of a nation, state, or community. Infrastructures are a community's basic physical and organizational structures that support human dignity and flourishing. Both must be in place to support the creation and growth of businesses in the private sector for sustainable human flourishing. When they are in place, the people tend to create the fruits of CREATE, OWN, and GROW. Chapter Fifteen identifies ten policies and infrastructures that must be in place to solve poverty.

7. To flourish, we should create the best value we can, own the best property we can, and grow the best business we can.

Creating value is an economically *virtuous action*. It creates new income.

Creating value and owning property is an economically *virtuous process*. The first creates income, and the second creates wealth.

Creating value, owning property, and growing business is an economically virtuous *cycle*.

Each action strengthens the following action. Once all three actions are in play, the collective effect is transformational. It maximizes our income and wealth. Then, the cycle can be repeated at a higher level, creating even more income and wealth. It can also repeat at higher levels of income and wealth in the next generations of our children and grandchildren if we intentionally teach them and if our children have the spirit to apply them.

Since business multiplies value and is the greatest engine of prosperity for nations, communities, families, and individuals, and since business is one of the most righteous things you can do, it is important to put the Biblical Wealth Engine # 3 GROW to work for you.

The statement of the practice of Wealth Engine #3 GROW is this: *Grow the best business you can.* Again, don't worry if you don't feel like an entrepreneur who can start or run a business. There are several ways to grow the best business you can, other than by being an entrepreneur, and one or more of them can fit your personality and gifts.

Chapter Thirteen will give you ten ways to grow the best business you can. It will give you different actions you can take and different roles you can play to do this.

The virtuous cycle of prosperity is possible anywhere a person has enough freedom to apply the wealth engines of CREATE, OWN, and GROW. It can take time to get each of them going, often years. But each one adds income, wealth, and opportunity, which grow as long as we keep trying to answer and act on these three questions:

- How can I create the best value?
- How can I own the best property?
- How can I grow the best business?

To move forward in growing the best business, you must rid your mind of a common fallacy. It is the fallacy that business is evil.

Business is not evil; I will explain why in the next chapter.

Chapter Twelve
The Business-is-Evil Fallacy

"I LEFT PASTORAL MINISTRY TO pursue my true calling of business," said almost no one in evangelical Christianity. Even when someone does this, they don't say it that clearly, and they often feel embarrassed and apologetic about it, as if it were a sin.

It doesn't fit the narrative of Christianity, which sees business as evil and ministry as good. Business is considered morally dirty, and those who do it are assumed to be morally corrupt or at least compromised. There is a similar narrative in the broader popular culture. It sees business as evil and almost anything else, like social work, teaching, working for the government, or art, as good and redeeming.

To see a culture's philosophy or moral judgments, look at its cartoons and stories for children. When was the last time you saw a cartoon depicting a businessperson as an honest and good person who was making the world a better place? It is rare. More common depictions are Mr. Burns on *The Simpsons* or Scrooge McDuck in *Duck Tales*.

Hollywood doesn't spend much time on movies portraying business or businesspeople as righteous. It prefers the evil narrative. It prefers storylines like *The Wolf of Wall Street*, the story of Jordan Belfort, played by Leonardo DiCaprio, who makes a fortune by defrauding investors.

Ebenezer Scrooge in Charles Dicken's *A Christmas Carol* is a classic example of the kind of businessman that some have come to associate with all businesspeople. Dicken describes him as "a squeezing, wrenching, grasping, scraping, clutching, covetous old sinner!"[30]

In Christian circles, a classic story of redemption is one of repentance of greed and materialism in business and a surrender of one's life to the work of pastoral or missionary service. I'm sure some have genuinely repented of greed and materialism and have been genuinely called by God into pastoral or missionary work, but has no one been called into the work of business? And have there not been greedy and materialistic pastors or missionaries? Are all businesspeople characterized by doing evil deeds?

THE SPIRIT OF CREATION

We made the biblical case for the righteousness of business in the last chapter. We have explained how the original human calling in Genesis 1:28 is to create new value in the world to make our living, serve others, make the world a better place, and worship God. We have explained how business creates that value on a multiplied scale. Since the essence of business is the multiplication of value on a multiplied scale, and since business funds every good thing, then doing business properly is one of the most righteous things we can do. God called Abraham our father in the faith. He and his next three generations were called to the work of business. And the rest of the Bible affirms the righteousness of business as a calling.

SO WHY IS THE FALLACY THAT BUSINESS IS EVIL SO PREVALENT? I SEE FOUR REASONS.

The first is the sin of envy. Envy is one of the darkest forces of the dark kingdom. It was Satan's motivation for rebelling against God. It was Satan's temptation to lure Adam and Eve into rebelling against God. It was Cain's motivation for murdering his brother Abel. And several of the Ten Commandments are in place to guard against the consequences of envying different things. Envy, for many of us, will be the reason we have our worst failings that hurt others the most and the reason others will hurt us the most. Envy is poison, and it ruins much.

Our sin nature is hard-wired to envy anyone who has more than us. Business owners can appear to have more than we do. We don't see their debt, and we don't see the pressures they face to stay in business, but we do see their businesses and the things that surround their lives, and they appear to have more than us. It is easy to assume that they have better lives than we do. And that feels unfair, so we ascribe the evils of greed and materialism to them to feel better about ourselves. That's pretty sick, but it is how our sin nature tries to jade reality in our minds. It's why we must renew our minds with the truth continuously.

The second is economic ignorance. Too many people think that money magically appears; we are all entitled to it and need a fair way to distribute it to everyone. Too many think the government magically creates this money by printing currency. These people believe in the zero-sum fallacy. They believe there is one limited, fixed, and puny pie of money, and we are all fighting against others for what we get. As we said in Chapter Six, they have pizza envy. Therefore, anyone who takes more than their fair share is an enemy of the people, and they believe business-people are the worst takers of unfair shares of the limited pie.

They don't understand that currency represents value, but the true value is in the products, services, and solutions that people create in the economy. If the government prints more money than is produced in these products, services, and solutions, the money gets diluted, and you get inflation. Irresponsible governments overproduce currency to tell their citizens the lie that they are giving them free money and programs when, in fact, they are stealing their money by giving them diluted value through higher prices.

The truth is that money in a free economy is a dynamic, ever-expanding pie. It grows constantly as people create new valued products, services, and solutions. Business is the organization of multiple people working together to multiply these things, which multiplies the creation of real money in the economy. Therefore, businesses are the mega-engines of prosperity, and businesspeople are the heroes of prosperity because they lead the multiplication of it. They are super-expanding the prosperity pie.

Third is Christian tunnel vision. In Chapter Three: "His Truth," we explained three kinds of tunnel vision in Christianity: Evangelical, New Testament, and Bible.

Evangelical Tunnel Vision is the belief that evangelism is our only purpose on earth. Thus, it sees everything else, like business, as a distraction at best and a sin at worst.

New Testament Tunnel Vision sees the New Testament as the only part of the Bible that is relevant for us to study in this age. That results in a narrow view of the Old Testament and its message of the value of business.

Bible Tunnel Vision sees the Bible as the only source of God's truth. That leads to ignorance of important subjects that make the righteous role of good business obvious. Subjects like history, political theory, and economics.

These tunnel visions together lead to a jaded view that the only purpose of life is to evangelize the lost. It misses the Cultural or First Commission God gave us in Genesis 1:28 to create value on earth. It also misses Jesus' teaching on the kingdom of God that we are to grow God's will in every sector of life and culture. And it misses having a biblical, logical, and historically grounded economic understanding. This tunnel vision leads to a lack of understanding that God calls many to business because business multiplies the fulfillment of the First Commission (Genesis 1:28); it funds every good thing, and if done properly, it is one of the most righteous things we can do.

The fourth is socialist power-mongering. Socialism is the ever-present political philosophy that claims to be from heaven but is from hell. It promises utopia and gives dystopia. Its essential fallacy is the fixed pie or the zero-sum fallacy. It views the economy as a war between everyone to divvy up a limited pie of resources. It makes liars, thieves, and weasels out of many. The worst weasels are the politicians in socialism because they are the true fat cats who benefit the most by controlling everything about the economy while they bleed everyone else. The essential fallacy of socialism is its atheistic view of man. It sees people as evolving animals trapped in a cage of meaningless labor who need socialist leaders to make the distribution of everything fair.

The real danger of socialism is its concentration of power with a few corrupted authorities in a central government. As Lord Acton said, "Power corrupts, and absolute power corrupts absolutely." Socialism demands absolute power because it is the only way it can force everyone to give up their freedoms.

Free business owners are the enemies of socialists because socialists believe they have stolen too much of the limited pie of the economy from everyone else and because their freedom and prosperity give them power that the socialists want to take for themselves and deny everyone else.

Hong Kong businessman Jimmy Lai is one modern example of a businessman who has run afoul of the socialists. Jimmy was smuggled out of communist China into British Hong Kong as a stowaway on a boat at the age of twelve in 1959. His family had been wealthy businesspeople in China, but all their wealth was confiscated during the Chinese Revolution under Mao. They were viewed as the enemy of the people who had stolen from the state. When Jimmy arrived in Hong Kong, he worked in a textile factory. It was long and hard work, but to Jimmy, it was wonderful to be out of communist China, making money, and having so many food options compared to what was available in China.

JOHN H. MORGAN

As Jimmy grew up, he moved up in the textile business and became an international textile sales representative. He read the economics classic, *The Road to Serfdom,* by F.A. Hayek, which changed his life. In one year, he got a big bonus from some large sales. He had been studying the stock market, and he took the risk of investing his bonus in it. His investments paid off, and he made a lot of money.

Jimmy started a clothing business with his new wealth, which he named Giordano, after eating at Giordano's Pizza in Chicago.

Those were the days of China's President Deng Xiaoping, who was reforming China's economy after Mao's death with more freedom for businesses. Jimmy expanded his clothing stores across China and made a fortune with quality, stylish clothing at fair prices. Unfortunately, the freedoms in China didn't last. The freedoms encouraged many Chinese to protest the government for even more freedoms. The Chinese government responded by harsh crackdowns on the protestors. The most famous was the Tiananmen Square Protests and shut down in 1989.

Jimmy Lai used his power and influence to advocate for freedom and criticize the Chinese government. He increased his activism by starting a media business called Next Media. It had a conservative daily newspaper called the Apple Daily, the most expensive and popular paper in Hong Kong.

The British handed Hong Kong over to the Chinese in 1997 after 156 years of rule in the former colony. The British had established a free economy and the rule of law in Hong Kong, which resulted in it becoming a modern, developed economy with thriving businesses. The Chinese government promised to honor a policy of one country with two systems for fifty years. They promised to allow Hong Kong to continue functioning with political and economic freedom and autonomy for that time. Many hoped fifty years would give the communist Chinese leaders in Beijing enough time to see the benefits of economic freedom in Hong Kong, to keep it in place, and possibly expand it in mainland China. However, they broke that promise and started to march toward totalitarian control of Hong Kong.

Jimmy Lai was vocal and active in the pro-democracy movement against the controls by Beijing and led many protests in Hong Kong. China enacted laws that increased Its control over free speech and dissent in Hong Kong. After one arrest and release, the communist Chinese government arrested Jimmy Lai at his home on December 31, 2020. They took him to the Next Media headquarters and perp-walked him in chains in front of all his staff as an act of humiliation and warning. They froze all his assets, as well as the assets of Next Media. Next Media stayed open as long as possible to speak out against the injustice, but it went broke and closed in June 2021.

Jimmy Lai was the son of a successful business family whom the communists in China ruined. He then became a very successful businessman, ruined by the Chinese Communists in Hong Kong. He claimed freedoms for his people and himself. He exercised free speech and criticized the government for its lies and unjust actions. That was the freedom the socialist communists would not and could not allow.

Jimmy Lai is a man of Christian faith. He had a calling to business. He provided jobs for thousands of people. He blessed the economies of China and Hong Kong. He used his calling to fight for freedom and human flourishing. He said he was willing to suffer for what was right, and he is.

Socialists call Jimmy Lai a thief and an enemy of the people. We call him a hero. You can see his story in the documentary film by the Acton Institute, *The Hong Konger: Jimmy Lai's Extraordinary Struggle for Freedom*, at https://thehongkongermovie.com. I encourage you to watch it, pray for Jimmy Lai to be freed, and advocate for his freedom.

To practice the Spirit of Creation and the Three Wealth Engines, you must rid your mind of the fallacy that business is evil. To do that, rid yourself of:

- Envy by focusing on the value you will create.
- Economic ignorance by embracing the Spirit of Creation.
- Christian Tunnel Vision by understanding the breadth of God's kingdom, his truth, and his calling.
- Socialist thinking by realizing it is based on the false beliefs that people are evolving animals whose material needs are best served by distributing the wealth of the limited fixed pie by a central powerful elite instead of the truth that people are created in the image of God, who flourish in freedom to constantly create new value, own property, and grow business.

You can't freely and fully grow a business if you don't believe it is righteous to do so.

YOU MUST REPLACE THE BUSINESS-IS-EVIL FALLACY WITH THE TRUTH. HERE ARE SEVERAL:

1. We are created in the image of God the Creator. (Genesis 1:26–27)
2. God's First Commission to us was to create new value on earth. (Genesis 1:28)
3. Business multiplies the fulfillment of the First Commission.
4. Business is the mega-engine of prosperity.
5. Business funds every good thing.
6. Business done properly is one of the most righteous things you can do.
7. To prosper, you should grow the best business you can.
8. If God has called you to business, accept that calling with humility, appreciation, and dedication.

Now that we have established the principle of Wealth Engine #3 GROW and have corrected the fallacy that business is evil, in the next chapter, we will teach ten ways to grow the best business you can.

Chapter Thirteen
Ten Ways to Grow the Best Business You Can

IT IS EARLY MORNING AS I write this section. In forty-five minutes, I will join an online meeting with a private equity team I am a partner with. We will discuss the guidance we will give later this morning to one of our clients who has the vision to grow his business in the hospitality space by ten times and to level up 13,000 employees in their life success. My role is to guide strategy, organizational structure, and design.

My life's work has been a struggle to decide if I am called to ministry or business. I left Dallas Theological Seminary as a young man before finishing a degree, partly because I felt so torn between the two. But then I promptly jumped into a full-time pastoral role because an opportunity arose that seemed to be God's leading. After five years, I left that and worked in business. At the same time, I finished a master's degree at Denver Seminary. After that, I took a pastorate for the next twenty-three years. During that pastorate, I led our church to make some strategic business moves that furthered the resources of the ministry; I developed a ministry to our business community and earned a Ph.D. in organizational leadership with a research emphasis in human capability and organizational design. In the last seven years of that pastorate, I founded People Prosper International to capitalize the Global Church to save souls, solve poverty, and change the world. Today, I lead PPI, a mixture of ministry, nonprofit work, and economic development, and I am a partner in a private equity firm that scales businesses.

As it turns out, my calling is at the intersection of ministry and business. I am called to both. I am called to do ministry with good business practices and business that grows the kingdom of Christ. Since business multiplies value, funds everything good thing in society, is one of the most righteous things you can do, and helps grow the kingdom of Christ, I thank God that I am called to business.

JOHN H. MORGAN

I understand the power of business to change your life and change the world, so I want to give you ten ways to grow the best business you can.

TEN WAYS TO GROW THE BEST BUSINESS YOU CAN

1. Think of Yourself as a Business Owner.

First, think of yourself as a business owner. See yourself as someone who *is* and who will be in business, even if you don't have a financial position in a business yet. The three major ways to have a financial position in business are as an *entrepreneur, an intrapreneur, or an investor.*

Entrepreneurs take calculated risks and invest some of their own money into starting and running a business. Intrapreneurs work as employees within a business, but they apply themselves as if they are owners to create value and grow that business. That usually results in them being promoted in that business and rewarded with higher pay and benefits. Sometimes, employees can receive 401Ks, which are investments in other businesses. They may also receive stock in their company or an equity position if their role and value-creation are high enough. The third way to grow the best business you can is as an investor. We will cover the role and activity of investing in business in number 10 below. Think of yourself as a business and as a business owner. Plan to be an entrepreneur, and/or an intrapreneur, and/or an investor.

2. Plan to Own and Grow a Business.

These are the steps to becoming an entrepreneur. Some of these steps will also apply to intrapreneurs who are seeking to improve and grow the businesses they work for.

Here are some planning steps to own and grow a business:

- Build equity in a property that you could use as collateral for a loan to start a business and/or save the money you can use to start a business.

- Be thinking about business ideas and opportunities that could work because they are needed, and for which you have the interest, knowledge, and skills. Answer the 6 "W Questions."

  - Who is your target market? Why do they need or want this? Will they pay what you need to charge to be profitable? And who is your competition? How do they operate, and how much of the market do they currently dominate? Can you beat your competition enough for the success you need? Is there room in your market for our business?
  - What is your business? What makes your business value proposition? What is the reason people will prefer your product or solution? Why will people choose your business over other options?
  - Where will you conduct your business: from home, from a business site, or online?
  - When will you conduct your business? One of my favorite restaurants is a little Cajun restaurant in Durango, Colorado. It is only open Thursday through Saturday nights for dinner and some select catering. The owner made a calculation on the most efficient use of all their business inputs and, frankly, how hard and long he wanted to work. And the place is killing it.
  - How will you conduct your business? The spirit with which you relate to your employees, colleagues, customers, and community is a huge factor in sustainable business growth and success. Everyone needs love and inspiration, and the best you can give it through your business while keeping the business functions running well, the more successful you will be. Regardless of what business you are in, you are ultimately in the people business.
  - Why are you compelled to start and run this business? If you don't love some significant things about this kind of business and work, you will not be able to sustain the energy it takes to succeed. You have to have the right why.

- Before you launch a business, you need a written and well-thought-out plan.

  You will have to have one if you are seeking a loan. If you are using your own money, you need it even more! If you need a business plan outline, search for one online. There are many options.

3. Start Your Business

A very important part of any endeavor is to start. It is an act of commitment and direction. I recommend you start by gaining the knowledge and skills needed in a particular business before you try to go full-time with your business. This is because the true knowledge of how to do every business comes from doing it. And you don't want to risk your income and wealth on the learning curve of something new. Here are several ways to do that.

Learn a business by working for someone else in that kind of business. This is an age-old method. It lets you grow your knowledge and skills in a particular business and see what works and what doesn't. As you do, you can see if you truly love that kind of business and have entrepreneurial juices or prefer to stay employed and work as an intrapreneur.

Start the business part-time as a side hustle. I did this with my nonprofit business, PPI. I started teaching the content that drives the organization while on mission trips as part of my former job as a pastor. Then I incorporated it as a nonprofit corporation and started building parts of the organization's programs while still pastoring. Then, I led our church through a pastoral succession and transitioned to PPI full-time when I knew it was time. The side-hustle PPI work was compatible with the missions goals of our church, and I negotiated the church's leadership succession and my work transition with our church board of directors. This allowed me to ramp up the learning curve and see if PPI could be an economically viable organization.

Take over someone's business who is ready to retire. This is another major way to own a business. Many people have built a business and are ready to retire in a few years, but they don't have children or existing employees who want to take over their business. My friends, Gary and Lisa just did this to become the owners of a beautiful plant nursery business in Colorado. They were on vacation and stopped by this business which they have loved over the years. They also happened to be at a time in their lives where they would like to leave their jobs, buy a business, and move from Texas to Colorado. They got into a conversation with the owners of the nursery who said they would like to retire soon, but they did not have anyone to take over their business. One thing led to another, and they negotiated a deal to transition the business from the owners to my friends. This one came by serendipity, but if you are looking for this kind of an opportunity, you can do two things. First, spread the word with as many people as possible to network with others who might know about opportunities. Second, contact some business brokers in the area where you would like to live and let them know the kind of business and deal you are looking for. Business brokers function like real estate brokers. They connect buyers and sellers and help complete the deal. In fact, some real estate brokers are also business brokers because their brokerage license allows them to do both in many states. If you are interested in this, start checking with real estate brokers to see if they have listings of businesses for sale.

According to Xavier Egan of the Minority Business Review, "Roughly 10 million small companies, or 65-75% of all small firms, will likely go up for sale in the next decade as baby boomers start to exit the marketplace."[31] This may be your golden opportunity to buy business.

Another way to start a business gradually is this. Start where you are with what you have and grow it organically. This goes back to the famous question that God asked Moses when he appeared to him in the desert. He asked him, "What's in your hand?" His shepherd's staff was symbolic of the leadership role that God was calling him to. And it would take God's power behind Moses to fulfill his calling.

So, what's in your hand? What's the best value you can create that others need? What do you know about, care about, and have the skills to create? This is how my friend, Banice Mburu in Kenya started what has now become Jade Collection, the premiere fashion store chain in Kenya with seven locations. Banice has always loved fashion, and as a young woman, she started selling ladies' scarves to secretaries in Nakuru and Nairobi offices. She kept growing her business one step at a time. She started by selling from office to office. Then, she sold them at a stall at a street market. Then, she opened her first modest store. Now, she has multiple stores, a dressmaking workshop, and a warehouse.

Here's a word of warning: Don't put your life savings or more debt than you can afford to lose into an unproven and untested business. It may be a great idea in your head, but the failure rate for new businesses, especially unproven businesses, is high. If you are taking over a proven business that you have made successful before, or if you have been running a new business long enough that you know it will make it, you can grow it by investing more money into it.

This doesn't mean you can't invest a large sum in a new business. It just means you must be very certain from experience that it has a high likelihood of succeeding and will keep your passion for making it succeed long enough to make it worth your investment of time, energy, and money.

4. Improve Your Business Systems.

It never ceases to amaze me how awful some businesses look, smell, and are run. The owners lose their desire to make more money by creating more value over time. My wife and I went to a restaurant that used to be known for how nice its franchises were, and it was in a nice strip mall. We ordered at a counter at the front of the restaurant. I had some clutter on it. But we ordered our food. As we headed back to the seating area, it got worse. The tables had a coat of sticky grime that we couldn't avoid. We tried several different tables with the same problem. It would take heavy stripping, sanding, and some new coats of finish to return those tables to decent and cleanable condition. It was just gross. We got our food, tried not to touch the table, and left, vowing never to eat there again. And it was clear that saying something to the manager was useless. Whoever owned it didn't care. They were content making a mediocre amount of money with less effort or didn't care that the business was dying.

If you want to grow your business, do more to improve your people, products, services, solutions, processes, and business systems.

5. Imitate what is working elsewhere and do it better.

If you have the temperament of a developer like me, you can't help but see how businesses and organizations do things well in other places and then try to imitate them in your organization. I am always looking for great ideas from any business or organization.

Back to my friend Banice Mburu of Jade Collection in Kenya. She saw the beautiful scarves she loved while on vacation in South Africa. She wondered why she could not find them in Kenya and bought as many as she could afford to bring home to see if she could sell them. And boom, they sold like hotcakes.

So, look for a business that is doing something you appreciate. You may be able to use it to improve your business, or it may be the beginning of a new business.

6. Innovate new products, services, and solutions.

One of the most powerful ways to grow a successful business is to innovate new products, services, and solutions. You either discover a new product or find a new way to deliver an old good thing. That's innovation, and it is the story of human progress.

One of my favorite new products from years back was the Keurig coffee pods coffee maker. It makes coffee taste better in individually brewed cups and easier to use than the old drip coffee makers. This innovation changed the coffee industry.

I also like how Chik Fil A innovated a fast and efficient multiple-line drive-through.

One of my favorite new solutions is a type of medical imaging that I had done that told me how much plaque was building up in my heart and arteries. Luckily, my plaque buildup was on the low end. My results indicate that I can take minor steps to help prevent heart disease.

Innovation of new products, services, or solutions sets you apart from your competition to grow your business. It'sher it is a simple or complex innovation, if it meets peoples' needs, it's going to grow your business.

7. Expand your business capacity.

If you have more demand for your business than you can deliver, it's time to expand your capacity. You can do that by adding one or more of these factors of capacity:

- Hire more people.

- Add technology that raises capacity.
- Hire people with higher capability to manage and lead.
- Add space.
- Increase your hours of operation.
- Buy equipment that will expand your capacity.
- Open another location for your business.
- Add another brand of your business for another market.

The Frontier Restaurant in Albuquerque has done all these things. Piece by piece, they expanded their space to include four commercial spaces next to their original space in a strip commercial building that takes a half block on Central Avenue across from the University of New Mexico in Albuquerque. They specialize in homestyle New Mexican food. They also bought a building behind their first building to serve as a prep kitchen and food storage facility. You have never seen a restaurant run the kind of volume they do in the space they have. It's like going to a theme park, but in a good way. They move many people through quickly and serve them awesome food. In addition, they have multiple other restaurants around Albuquerque called Golden Pride Chicken, which features fried chicken and more New Mexican food. It is a money-making empire because it serves great food with good service and keeps expanding its capacity to meet demand. Writing this makes me hungry for their breakfast of fried eggs with fried potatoes smothered in New Mexico green chile, a homemade tortilla on the side, and a shared breakfast desert of their famous cinnamon rolls. It's money. Literally.

This is when you should consider taking out a loan to expand your business. You have proven the business model. You know your financials. You have more demand than you can fulfill.

Expand your capacity to meet your demand.

8. Expand your business demand.

You may have the opposite problem because most businesses do. You may have more capacity to sell and deliver products, services, and solutions than you have demand. You may need more customers and more business.

If that's the case, you need to grow your demand by improving the quality of your business experience. You should grow organically and then increase people's awareness of how great it is. Make it great, then promote it like crazy.

If you make it great, your customers will help spread the word. Then, when you promote it, your promotions will pay off with return customers.

9. Create another business.

Some people get one business going well and then gain an interest in and vision to start a different one. They use principles and practices that they have learned in one business to help them succeed in another one. They might use some of their profits or equity in their first business to help start their next one. These people are corporate entrepreneurs, meaning they create a body or a corporate system of several businesses under the umbrella of their leadership.

It's not for everyone, but for the ones who are gifted and called to it, it's a fit. The power of it is that one can create a virtuous cycle of value creation with multiple businesses. If you add to that the ownership of multiple properties and the continual personal growth of the top leader to keep creating the best value he or she can, it maximizes the virtuous cycle of value and wealth creation.

There are two keys to owning and running multiple businesses. First, you must give clear directional leadership for the kind and culture of your businesses. Second, you must place a great manager, GM, or CEO leading each business. That means your top business unit executive has the mental capacity to manage your business, the knowledge and skills to manage it well, the desire to manage it well, and an absence of sabotaging behaviors like addiction, a lack of integrity, or poor people skills.

If you have one business going well and want to start another one, find a great manager, give him or her great direction and support, and give them enough running room to succeed.

10. Invest in Business.

The tenth way to grow the best business you can is to invest in one or more. Doing this lets you own a piece of the business(es). As business value grows, your investment grows. Just about everyone should be an investor in business.

The stock market is a market for investing in businesses. Of course, the market goes up and down, but its long-term return has averaged approximately 9% per year.[32] Compounded over time, that is significant

Some people falsely claim that investing in the stock market is a gamble, just like gambling at a casino in Las Vegas. That is not true. Gambling at a casino is based on sheer random odds, and the games are tilted to win for the house in the long run. It's how they pay for themselves.

The stock market is based on businesses run by people who intentionally work to create value to make a profit. Intentional rational people created in the image of God are not like random dice, cards, or slot machines They are the agents of value creation. That means staying out of casinos and investing in good businesses is a wise choice. I recommend investing in a market index fund like one that invests in the S&P 500. If you have a 401K with your job, it gets invested in businesses in the market. It is probably managed by an investment firm that manages what funds and businesses it is invested in.

Investing in a private equity fund is another way of investing in businesses. Private equity businesses raise private equity funds to invest in businesses and they sometimes help manage them to create the returns they seek. The average return from 1986 to 2022 in private equity was 14.28%.[33]

The Securities and Exchange Commission rules for private equity investment have blocked most investors from participating. The rules have generally been that one has to be an accredited investor. That means an investor with $1 million or more in assets other than the equity in their home. However, there is a bill in Congress to expand access to private equity investment to more people. We will see where that goes. Hopefully, it will succeed.

Tony Robins recently released his book *The Holy Grail of Investing: The World's Greatest Investors Reveal their Ultimate Strategies for Financial Freedom*. In it, he makes the case for private equity investing. He states that he didn't even know about it for much of his life, but it is the investment his wealthiest friends use to grow their wealth. Now, he is a partner in an investment firm specializing in private equity investing.

HERE AGAIN, ARE THE TEN WAYS TO GROW THE BEST BUSINESS YOU CAN:

1. Think of Yourself as a Business Owner.
2. Plan to Own and Grow a Business.
3. Start Your Business.
4. Improve Your Business Systems.
5. Imitate what is working elsewhere and do it better.
6. Innovate new products, services, and solutions.
7. Expand your business capacity.
8. Expand your business demand.
9. Create another business.
10. Invest in business.

You can't do all of these at once, but you can pick which of these ten ways to create the best business you can is your top priority. Circle the one that you need to focus on now and do it. Then, move on to the next one and do it. And keep doing that.

SECTION SUMMARY

The big idea in the first section from Chapters One through Thirteen is that there is an economic worldview based on sound economics, historical evidence, and biblical teaching that we call the Spirit of Creation. The Spirit of Creation is the root cause of prosperity, and the absence of it is the root cause of poverty.

The foundational ideas of the Spirit of Creation are the Three Biblical Wealth Engines.

They are:

Wealth Engine #1 CREATE. Value is created, so we should create the best value we can.

Wealth Engine #2 OWN. Property preserves value, so we should own the best property we can.

Wealth Engine #3 GROW. Business multiplies value, so we should grow the best business we can.

Here it is in a big-picture diagram.

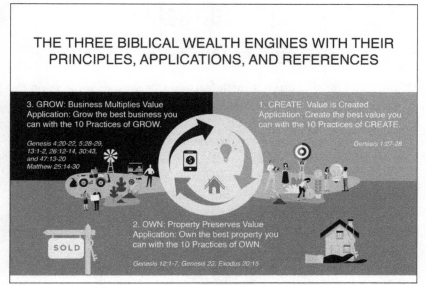

THE THREE BIBLICAL WEALTH ENGINES WITH THEIR
PRINCIPLES, APPLICATIONS, AND REFERENCES

3. GROW: Business Multiplies Value
Application: Grow the best business you
can with the 10 Practices of GROW.

Genesis 4:20-22, 5:28-29,
13:1-2, 26:12-14, 30:43,
and 47:13-20
Matthew 25:14-30

1. CREATE: Value is Created
Application: Create the best value you
can with the 10 Practices of CREATE.

Genesis 1:27-28

2. OWN: Property Preserves Value
Application: Own the best property you
can with the 10 Practices of OWN.

Genesis 12:1-7, Genesis 23, Exodus 20:15

SOLD

The Three Biblical Wealth Engines, Expanded

In the next section, we address the book's promised outcomes: How to Fund Your Calling, Solve Poverty, and Capitalize the Global Church. Big promises, indeed! It will also include a chapter on Charity, Responsibility, Empowerment, and Partnership and a final chapter titled Go Forth and Conquer!

Now that you understand the Spirit of Creation let's put it to work.

Chapter Fourteen
Fund Your Calling

I LOOKED DOWN THE ROCK drop-off with fear and trepidation. We were on the Alien Trail in northwest New Mexico, just north of the city of Aztec. My friend, James, watched from below with a sly grin. I would either make it or crash and burn, but my pride would not let me dismount and hike down. "Just lean back," he said, "and trust your wheels to roll through it."

I released the brakes on my mountain bike and dropped in. I thought I was going over the handlebars, but before I knew it, I was through the drop-off and fighting for balance to stay on the trail below and not go off a ledge. I skidded to a stop next to James. He rumbled with his infectious laugh. I laughed in relief and vented some fear. He probably would have laughed even more if I had crashed. Such is male friendship.

James became my good friend and mountain bike coach, and he and his wife are valued partners in our work at PPI. I love James and Rose for several reasons. One of them is how they have grown in living out their salvation, callings, and economic empowerment through surrender to Christ.

James is part Hopi and part Navajo. Rose is Navajo. When they started visiting our church in Farmington, New Mexico, they were a young couple living together and struggling in several ways. They were struggling for peace in their hearts as they had family histories of alcoholism and abuse. They were struggling in their relationship with each other. They were struggling with their sense of work and purpose. And they were struggling economically.

Then, they heard how surrendering their lives to Christ could bring God's salvation and blessings into their lives. They made that decision of faith and started their spiritual journey of growing in their relationship with him.

They began relating to each other with more patience and grace. They decided to step away from a life of alcohol abuse. They got married, and I had the privilege of officiating their wedding at their house. They gave me a Pendleton Cayuse Indian Blanket as a thank-you gift, which has stayed on my side of our bed ever since. It protects me from the freezing temperatures my wife likes to set in our house at night. You could hang meat in our house at night, but that is another story.

They took steps of faith to grow in their careers. James had been working as a school custodian and was known for his crazy sense of humor. Rose saw an advertisement for a standup comedy competition, and she challenged James to enter it, which he did. He was very nervous but settled into his routine and killed it. He won the contest, and the rest is history.

James has become a famous Native American comedian, actor, motivational speaker, spokesperson, and life success coach. He is an overcomer in multiple ways, including his two recoveries from bouts of cancer that included major surgeries. James' hobby is competitive mountain biking, and he advocates for healthy lifestyles.

James travels across the U.S. and Canada, speaking for Native tribal groups on hundreds of tribal reservations. Rose is James' manager, and she has developed a merchandising business that features their Warrior Strong brand and a line of Native American crafts.

They have a good marriage and good kids, have bought a lovely home, have good businesses, and live and work with a sense of God's purpose and calling. God's salvation, calling on their lives, and funding of their callings through His Spirit of Creation are all woven together, as they are for everyone who will surrender to Christ in these areas.

So, this chapter answers the question: How does the Spirit of Creation fund our callings? Here is the answer. The Spirit of Creation funds your calling through the CREATE, OWN, and GROW actions through one or more jobs in one or more organizations as God leads you.

Here are four major steps to work this out.

FIRST, CLARIFY YOUR CALLING

The three calling questions are deceptively powerful and can create some anxiety because honesty in answering them can cause a lot of upheaval in our lives. But I would challenge you to answer these questions in good faith that God is working in your heart to create righteous desires that fit his purpose for you.

This must be understood with spiritual maturity. A false or immature understanding of this leads to the false belief that whatever we desire is God's calling, and that creates a world of relativism where we become our own gods, and we become the measure of truth. We baptize our sinful desires and lusts and call it God's will. And that is the road to destruction.

So, this is a dangerous truth. In the hands of a person like the great missionary William Carey, it becomes the righteous desire to share Jesus with those who have not heard of him on the far side of the world. In the hands of an unbeliever, a false believer, or an immature believer, it can become their way to justify every desire, lust, obsession, delusion, pathology, and sin. It creates monsters in the name of God.

In Philippians 2:12-13, the Apostle Paul, under the inspiration of the Holy Spirit, tells the Philippian believers,

> *Therefore, my dear friends, as you have always obeyed – not only in my presence, but how much more in my absence – continue to work out your salvation with fear and trembling, for it is God who works in you to will and to act according to his good purpose.*

The admonition is not to work *for* our salvation but to work *out* our salvation. The latter means to work out the processes of who we are in Christ. Our salvation is both a transactional point-in-time event with God by faith and a continual process of growth and development in Christ. Works do not save us, but living out our faith and salvation is a long work process.

God leads us in his progressive work in us, and we must follow.

God is giving us righteous desires that fit his calling on our lives. He is at work in us to give us the will, which is the desire. God's Spirit is giving us some righteous desires.

God is also giving us some abilities. He is at work in us to will and to act on his good pleasure. He gives us the "want to" and the "can do." The Bible affirms that God created us to do his work on earth through his leading and empowering, but we must be deeply connected to Him to be on our true calling and with his empowering grace.

This is dangerous and scary. Earlier in my Christian life, I thought Paul's language of calling this process one of "fear and trembling" was hyperbole. But now that I have lived it, that is exactly what it entails. Most Christians do not honestly ask and answer the three WHAT, WHY, and HOW questions at a deep spiritual level because it is too scary. The answer would upheave their lives too much. The answer would cause more risk than they want to take. I don't think you have truly heard your calling if it does not cause some fear and trembling. It is the nature of God's plan for us to trust in him by faith to do his will. Who in the Bible heard the call of God and was not initially struck by fear and trembling?

So, my challenge is to dig deep into your relationship with God and, with your most sincere surrender to Christ, ask him what the most righteous desires are that he is placing in your heart. Ask his Spirit to fill your spirit with the answers to the WHAT, WHY, and HOW calling questions. Spend time with God, write out your answers, and keep editing them until you have them concisely. When it is 100% true to God's calling and your gifts, as best as you can tell with your purest motivation, and when it causes you fear and trembling, you are getting close.

The calling questions are:

- What do I love to create?
- Why do I love to create it?
- How do I love to create it?

Take some time to write out your answers, then commit to returning to these questions and rewriting them as God gives you more clarity. Keep growing in the clarity of your calling.

Here are my WHAT, WHY, and HOW answers.

What I love to create:

I love to curate and communicate transformational truths at the intersection of theology, leadership, and economics and to develop the breakthrough high-growth phase of organizations that fulfill those truths.

Why I love to create it:

It uses my gifts to unleash other people's callings to grow the kingdom of God.

How I love to create it:

- Through thought and directional leadership.
- By influencing ministries, nonprofits, and businesses.
- With a global vision of growing Christ's kingdom.
- By doing 80% deep work and 20% team and public work.

Every step to follow Christ more clearly in my calling has been scary. Stating my current calling WHAT, WHY, and HOW answers here is scary because acting on them more in the ways God is leading me will cause new levels of risk and faith—fear and trembling, indeed.

Your calling can be simpler than mine or my friend James's. Every calling in God's plan is important and has eternal value. But the first step is to clarify it.

SECOND, LET YOUR CALLING SHAPE YOUR CREATE, OWN, AND GROW ACTIONS

We spent the first thirteen chapters of this book teaching you the Spirit of Creation that results in a lifestyle of asking these three economic action questions:

- How can I create the best value?
- How can I own the best property?
- How can I grow the best business?

Now, we are saying that your calling needs to shape your answers to these questions. So, they become these questions:

- How do I create the best value on my calling? That means what is the best job, jobs, or business(es) I could have to create the best value I can on my calling?

- How do I own the best property on my calling? What kind of home and where would help fulfill my calling? What kind of income, investment, or business/organization property would help fulfill my calling?
- How do I grow the best business(es) on my calling? Should I be an entrepreneur, an intrapreneur, or an investor? Should I have a combination of these roles?

THIRD, SEEK THE JOBS AND ORGANIZATIONS THAT BEST FIT YOUR CALLING

The question is, should I work in one job or two or several? Most people work in one job and for one organization at a time. But God is creative, and so are combinations of jobs and organizations to which he leads some of his people.

A biblical example was the Apostle Paul. He worked as an apostle/ missionary and sometimes as a tentmaker. He did his missionary work full-time when he had enough support from the people he ministered to. He would add his tentmaking work when he needed to create income to support his core calling or when he needed to make a point about the righteousness of honest work to make one's living. God providentially gave him the talents, knowledge, and skills for both works, and he used them for his whole life calling.

Another example is a couple we know who went to China under a special visa where the husband worked as a veterinarian. His core calling was to do Christian missionary work of evangelism and discipleship, but he used his profession as a means of living in China and supporting his family and ministry. Those two works are not very similar, but one supported the other. That's okay. God used that combination of work to fulfill their whole life callings.

This model of multiple jobs for ministers, or tentmaking, makes sense for many pastors and missionaries in the Majority Church. Since many of the Majority World churches and organizations do not have fully developed Spirit of Creation ecosystems where their people have the means to support them fully, an alternative is to equip their pastors and missionaries with professions or small businesses where they can make their livings to support their core callings of ministry work. One small business system we have seen is equipping a pastor or missionary with the capital, knowledge, and skills to run a transportation business. They can get a vehicle like a motorcycle or a tuk-tuk, a three-wheeler, and be the driver, or they can build and manage a business of several vehicles with hired drivers. They repay their business loan, fund their lives, and fund their ministries with the income from the business. Another common model is for the pastors or missionaries to make some income from their church, some from farming, and some from a school they start and operate in connection with their church.

In Chapter Sixteen, we teach how to Capitalize the Global Church. Pastors and missionaries in high-poverty regions must be able to make their living as tentmakers while also leading the process of capitalizing their Christian communities with the Spirit of Creation. As the Spirit of Creation takes root and grows, they will rise in economic income and wealth and be able to support their pastors and missionaries full-time. However, they must lead that biblical economic empowerment process, or the next generation will have the same problem.

Supporting pastors and missionaries full-time is not feasible in high-poverty spaces. There must be a developmental process of growing from one step to another. For Christian ministers, it starts with working as tentmakers and teachers of the Spirit of Creation in one generation, then moving up to the full-time support of ministers in the next. The problem is that often, western missionaries pushed national ministers to live on ministry support only when that was not sufficient for their needs and when there was no teaching of the Spirit of Creation to create economic empowerment for the Christian communities. In the worst cases, western missionaries criticized the national pastors for trying to make their livings in secular jobs while also serving in their ministries. It is an unrealistic and unbiblical expectation.

Some people's whole life calling leads them to work in several jobs and organizations. They may use a combination of professional work, businesses, ministries, and nonprofits to do their WHAT, WHY, and HOW work and their CREATE, OWN, and GROW work.

One historical example was the great missionary William Carey. He started in England with two jobs. He was a cobbler and a pastor. He supported himself from both, but pastoring was his core calling. He sailed to India in 1793 with his family and became the first of many who ventured out, igniting the modern missions movement. His combination of works throughout his life in India included evangelism and discipleship, managing an indigo business, starting a school for the children of British expatriates, starting a school for poor Indian children, farming, starting the Agricultural Society of Bengal, starting the Agri-Horticultural Society of India in Calcutta, mastering Bengali, Sanskrit and other languages, starting the first Indian degree-awarding college at Serampore, and teaching at Fort William College in Calcutta.

Carey had raised enough money in England for his passage to India and three months of support to give him time to establish himself in some income-producing work. He had different combinations of work at different times. Sometimes they seemed similar, and sometimes they seemed different. All his works, except his missionary work, produced income that supported his missionary work. God was using the gifts, interests, and talents he had given Carey to work out his whole life calling. His whole life calling resulted in 700 converts to Christianity, the Bible being translated into Bengali, Sanskrit, Hindi, and three other languages, the translation of some Hindu classics into English, his campaign against the Indian custom of burning widows to death on their husband's funeral pyres, and his advocacy against the caste system. His greatest achievements were being the Father of Modern Missions, a movement that changed the world, and the pioneer missionary to India who created a wave of missionaries that followed and created a Christian movement in India.[34]

A modern example is my friend, Tim. Tim's core calling is to do three things: unleash people's callings, connect people strategically, and help leaders scale their businesses. He does that through multiple businesses and jobs. He is the principal founder of three private equity firms — two focus on scaling real estate investments and one on scaling lower middle market companies. Tim has several other businesses and is an advisor to several. He is called to grow the kingdom of Christ through business, and the structure that best fits his calling is a body of several jobs in several organizations. As he does his business work, Tim is constantly witnessing how Christ is the center of his life, and he encourages others to make Christ the center of their lives.

The Spirit of Creation is also the way to fund organizations. An organization may fulfill its calling or mission and create its funding in the structure of one organization. Most do.

An organization may fulfill it in two organizations. One may focus more on the mission, and the other may focus more on creating revenue. An example is the Kasr El Dobara Evangelical Church in Cairo, Egypt, the largest evangelical church in Egypt and the Arab world, according to its website. Its Beit El Wadi conference and training center south of Cairo at Wadi El Natroun is both a ministry center and an economic income generator for the whole ministry.

Then, some become a body of several organizations in the technical sense of the term corporation, which comes from the word body. It takes multiple organizations to fulfill and fund their full calling or mission. They may be a body of businesses and/or nonprofits that all work toward a common mission.

An example of this is Buckner International, a Texas-based nonprofit that fulfills its mission through its nonprofit organization, through mission-oriented and revenue-creating organizations, like their senior living communities, and through economic development projects in the six foreign countries where it operates. They influence governments for good policies, like placing orphaned children with some of their extended families rather than in orphanages or in even worse places that resemble prisons. They receive some of their funding to help deliver government-approved services to low-income families and individuals from the government. They operate across the spectrum of nonprofits, businesses, and governments, with an impressive kingdom impact on many people.

So, seek your best job or jobs in one or more organizations that fit your calling, as God works in you to will and to act for his good purposes. Don't put yourself mentally in a box of limitations that do not exist. "The earth is the Lord's and everything in it. Its people and all who dwell in it," (Psalm 24:1). This includes all forms of organizations. Use the combination in your jobs and organizations that fit your calling and God's leading.

FOURTH, STEWARD YOUR INCOME AND RESOURCES WELL ON YOUR CALLING

Here are three major components of this stewardship.

First, Develop income drivers. Look at your role(s) and organization(s) and determine your best income drivers and grow them. Just because you are on your mission from God does not mean you get a pass on good resource stewardship. You must create them by creating value that generates income. And you must sell it because nothing sells itself. Even the gospel must be proclaimed to have effect. So, you must proclaim the value you are providing and sell it compellingly.

Second, be frugal. Don't spend money where it is not needed. Don't spend to impress people. If you impress people, impress them with your security in who you are, the value of your calling, and your financial stewardship.

Third, deploy your resources effectively. Hire people who bring high value to your organization. Buy equipment and supplies wisely for what they can do to fulfill and fund your calling in the long run. Buy property for your organization's long-term financial sustainability and strength. And develop businesses, if it fits, to create revenue for your mission.

Norm Brodsky, a successful entrepreneur and senior columnist for Inc. Magazine, frequently said in his articles that the number one reason new businesses fail is because they run out of money before they break even and start making money. At both the personal and organizational levels, we must develop our income drivers, be frugal, and deploy our resources effectively. If we don't, we won't have the resources we need for our lives or callings.

SUMMARY

In summary, the Spirit of Creation funds your calling as the What, Why, and How of your calling shapes your CREATE, OWN, and GROW actions through one or more jobs in one or more organizations as God leads you.

The Spirit of Creation Funds Your Calling As…

The scriptures say, "My God shall supply all your needs according to his riches in glory by Christ Jesus," (Philippians 4:19). That doesn't mean that God drops everything in our laps while we sit on our backsides. It means we do the CREATE, OWN, and GROW work prescribed in the Bible on the callings that God has given us and in the jobs and organizations that he leads us to, and he blesses the work of our hands with opportunities and success.

We need to clarify our callings, let our callings shape our economic actions, seek the best jobs and organizations, and steward our resources well.

That is how the Spirit of Creation funds our callings. The next big promise of this book is how the Spirit of Creation solves poverty.

A big promise, indeed.

Chapter Fifteen
Solve Poverty

NOW, WE COME TO THE second major promised outcome of this book: the answer to how to solve poverty. It is a subject where angels fear to tread. At the risk of sounding foolish, we advocate for the school of thought that the best way to solve poverty is to identify its root causes and then work systematically to change those causes. The evidence shows that poverty is caused by the lack of the conditions that create prosperity.

From some of the best practitioners, researchers, and thought leaders on the issues of poverty and prosperity, I see four conditions that create prosperity. I believe they are the cure for poverty. The best way to explain it is with a metaphor I call The Tree of Life.

THE TREE OF LIFE THAT SOLVES POVERTY AND CREATES HUMAN FLOURISHING

4. The **fruit** is the spiritual, social, and material wealth created by the people.

3. The **branches** are the 10 infrastructures that support the Spirit of Creation.

2. The **trunk** is the 10 policies that support the Spirit of Creation.

1. The **roots** are the critical mass of people who possess the Spirit of Creation.

The Tree of Life

The tree of life in the books of Genesis and Revelation refers to the eternal life-giving relationship with God. The book of Proverbs uses it as a metaphor for the blessings that come in this life from living in God's wisdom. We use the term here in the general sense of God's blessings.

Our Tree of Life illustration gives the four conditions that solve poverty and create human flourishing. Here are the explanations of each of them.

#1. THE ROOTS ARE A CRITICAL MASS OF PEOPLE WHO POSSESS THE SPIRIT OF CREATION

The Spirit of Creation is the opposite of the spirit of poverty. It is the root solution to the root cause of poverty. When a critical mass of the Spirit of Creation exists in a culture, the people naturally begin to create value that creates new income, own property that preserves and grows value, and grow businesses that multiply value and wealth. They are also prone to develop the policies and infrastructures that support those activities.

Nothing can replace or rival the power of The Spirit of Creation in culture to create human prosperity. It is the root of the personal, cultural, and national Tree of Life. All other treatments can be applied, except this, and they will not last because they don't align with the timeless principles of human flourishing. Sooner or later, they will create trees with little or no fruit.

The Spirit of Creation in a culture directs the people to do what it takes to build a flourishing economy. It directs them to good economic activity, policies, and development.

Michael Matheson is the director and producer of the documentary *Poverty, Inc.*, the DVD series *PovertyCure*, and the *Good Society Series*. He points out that most thought about and practice of poverty amelioration centers around the next two factors of good policies and infrastructures, but few ask the deeper questions of what kind of culture gives rise to them. He makes the case that Christianity provided the cultural roots for the activities, policies, and infrastructures that created prosperity in the West.[35] We agree and coin that particular part of the Christian worldview, the Spirit of Creation.

Miller points out three cultural ideas rooted in the Bible that came from the Judeo-Christian worldview and gave rise to the scientific innovations and economic revolution of prosperity in the West.

First is the concept of linear time. Most other cultures saw time as circular and the earth as eternal. Christianity sees time as linear and the earth as temporal, with it all leading to a culminating purpose of God. This gave rise to a higher purpose for human life and an emphasis on progress towards God's purposes.

Second, is the concept of people being created in the image of the Creator with a commission to continue creating value on earth. This contrasted with the common pagan view that work was a necessary evil to be avoided whenever possible.

The third concept was the goodness and knowability of nature, in contrast to the view that nature was evil, capricious, and unknowable. This concept led to the scientific revolution, which improved the conditions of human life dramatically.[36]

Miller argues, as historian and sociologist Christopher Dawson did, "that the driving force of culture is not the economy or politics but *cultus* – religion."[37] He concludes, "I am asserting that without these fundamental ideas of linear time, the goodness and intelligibility of the natural world, and the dignity of man and labor, we would not have seen the scientific or economic developments that have characterized the West and that frankly have become the models for progress in non-Western contexts."[38]

I believe a critical mass of people who possess the Spirit of Creation, or the lack of it, is the root cause of prosperity or poverty in a culture. A critical mass that has it eventually leads to policies and infrastructures that support it and further human flourishing.

By critical mass, we mean enough people possess the Spirit of Creation to create a self-sustainable and growing movement to create the four conditions of the Tree of Life. It does not require a majority of the population to create a movement. Like most historical movements, it can start with a small minority of highly committed people and grow to change a culture. As the cultural anthropologist Margaret Mead said, "Never doubt that a small group of thoughtful, committed citizens can change the world: indeed, it's the only thing that ever has."[39] The Jesus movement is a prime example.

The next factor in solving poverty is policies that support people in practicing the actions of the Spirit of Creation, which are CREATE,

OWN, and GROW. We identify ten policies that support the Spirit of Creation as the trunk of the Tree of Life.

#2. THE TRUNK IS THE TEN POLICIES THAT SUPPORT THE SPIRIT OF CREATION

The Spirit of Creation provides a sound political-economic-theological philosophy among the people so that they enact good laws that promote prosperity and avoid bad ones that promote poverty. How nations organize and run their affairs is called their political economy. Their philosophy of politics, economics, and theology are bound together. As goes their metaphysics or religion, so goes their politics, and as goes their politics, so goes their economics. Then, as goes their economics, so goes their prosperity or poverty.

In our metaphor, good policies that support the Spirit of Creation are the trunk of the tree of life. They translate the principles of human flourishing from the roots into good laws. Here are ten policies that support the Spirit of Creation.

1. Freedom.

The first principle is freedom: religious, political, and economic. It is rooted in the conviction that people have God-given rights to life, liberty, and the pursuit of happiness and that it is the government's first purpose to protect these rights.

The thought leader and diplomat Michael Novak wrote over forty books on the philosophy and theology of culture. His most noted work was *The Spirit of Democratic Capitalism*. His thesis was that culture must have three requisite freedoms for lasting and true freedom, justice, and prosperity. He likened them to the three requisite legs for a stool. Those freedoms are religious, political, and economic freedom. They are in that order of priority, and the existence of each one ensures the existence of the other two. The absence of one of them leads to the absence of the other two. Thus, his title *The Spirit* (religious liberty) *of Democratic* (political liberty) *Capitalism* (economic liberty).

2. The Rule of Law.

The rule of law means that good laws are enacted in an open, democratic, and fair process and applied evenly to everyone. It is the opposite of the rule of man, which means that powerful people get to live by their own rules or force their unfair rules on others.

Practically, it means the police do not stop you and try to shake you down for a bribe, as I have experienced in Latin America and Haiti. It means if the judge of a trial you are in is a member of a rival tribe, he or she will not use that animus to rule against you. It means when you go to a government agency to get a permit to build a well, house, or school, they don't shake you down for a bribe, which is common in the poverty world. It means that powerful public officials or a favored class of people don't get to break the law without suffering the same consequences as others.

When you understand the rule of law, you realize we live in a corrupt world. And corruption has a high economic cost. The more it costs, the less people make the effort, and the less people will make the effort to create value, the less value is created.

3. Limited Government.

The government is like the invasive vine called Kudzu, in the U.S. South. It tends toward overgrowth, overreach, and tyranny. The check on this tyranny is to keep the government limited to its key roles.

The classic book on this topic is F. A. Hayek's *The Road to Serfdom*. His thesis was that by both good and foul intent, governments tend to grow with more laws, regulations, and taxation. Although it seems justifiable when considered by itself, each new law, regulation, and tax is one more encroachment on personal liberties. Eventually, that process of government creep turns the people into slaves to it.

Hayek argued that the most constant and present danger to liberty is one's own government and that constant vigilance must be paid to keep one's government focused and limited to its essential purposes.

The American founders believed the essential purpose of government was to ensure its people's rights to life, liberty, property, and the pursuit of happiness. Since its founding, the American government and many state, county, and city governments have gone way beyond this mandate to create laws, regulations, and taxation to try to fix every problem any legislator thought they needed to please themselves or their constituents. This Kudzu of government creep is way out of hand and needs serious pruning and growth control. Too many programs favor one class of people at the expense of others, one industry and kind of business at the expense of others, and foreign aid at the expense of all citizens. It gets paid by taxes on income, capital gains, business profits, licenses, permits, tolls, purchases, uses, property, and death! As President Ronald Reagan used to say, the Democrats' view of taxation is that if something moves, tax it. If it continues to move, tax it more. If it quits moving, subsidize it.

If we don't limit government, we will be slaves to it, and the cost of that slavery will suppress our ability to create prosperity.

4. Marriage and Family.

The family is society's primary institution; marriage is its first and most important relationship, and raising children by their parents is its most important task. No culture can survive with good character and sustainable prosperity without these priorities.

The culture of marriage and child-raising also has economic benefits for the family members and society. Generally, married men and women make more money and create more wealth over time than single adults. Their family responsibilities focus their attention and discipline on good work. It is also because the family becomes an economic unit that creates an economy of scale in their housing, food, and other needs. They share the expenses and benefits of living together. Children from intact families with engaged fathers and mothers tend to do better economically and socially.

Pope John Paul II's book on the family is called *Love and Responsibility*. In it, he says that the family is the school of love. People learn to do what is in the best interests of others. As we learn to love our family members, we learn to love others in society, which is an essential social need for human flourishing. It creates trust, care, and peace. The opposite is a brutal spirit of hyper-competition, jealousy, envy, anger, abuse, hatred, crime, and war.

5. Human Equality.

All people are created in God's image and are ontologically equal. Ontological means in the essence of one's being.

That is why the Christian ethic treats everyone with dignity and equality, which includes the right to work, to own property, and to grow a business.

Equality is also an economic benefit because it allows everyone access to the activities of economic flourishing. The more people do these economic activities, the more the economy grows, creating opportunities for individuals to CREATE, OWN, and GROW. If everyone has a chance to work or start a business, you have more people to buy your products or create businesses that could offer you a job.

Equality is good economics, and it helps solve poverty. When women can access economic opportunities, it lifts them, their children, and their husbands. The Proverbs 31 woman with multiple economic enterprises had a husband elevated as an elder in the city gates. Her win was also his win.

When people of both genders and all ethnicities and religions have access to economic opportunities, everyone wins and has a better economy. Everyone has more customers who can buy what they create, and everyone has more options for goods, services, and solutions to buy.

6. Property Rights.

Property rights mean people have the legal right to buy or legally acquire property, to use it for legal purposes, and to sell it as they wish. The government or others may not confiscate it without an overwhelmingly just cause and fair compensation.

The global expert on the role of property rights in solving poverty is a Peruvian economist, Hernando De Soto. He is also the president of the Institute for Liberty and Democracy in Lima, Peru. His book *The Mystery of Capital: Why Capitalism Triumphs in the West and Fail Everywhere Else* makes the case that the difference between the poor and the non-poor of the world is that the non-poor own property legally, and the poor do not. The poor generally live in places with little or no property rights. So, a primary step in solving poverty is to create property rights.

Some of the characteristics of property rights are these:

- A government entity keeps accurate, accessible, affordable property ownership records.
- It is easy, efficient, and affordable for individuals to buy or sell properties legally, for the buyer's ownership to be recorded, and for them to receive a legal deed.
- Financial service businesses can operate to lend property purchase loans at an affordable price.
- Laws protect property owners from squatters, vandals, thieves, or unjust and unfair government expropriation.
- Courts defend the rights of property owners.
- Law enforcement officials enforce the laws to protect property owners.
- Property taxes are zero or low amounts that do not, in effect, expropriate property.

Several years ago, I had a tenant renting a small property I owned. She let her boyfriend, who had just gotten out of jail, move in with her, and they both descended into a life of drug addiction and not paying their rent. I gave them the legal notices required by law to pay their rent, or I would take them to court to be evicted. They continued not to pay their rent, and we went to court. The judge asked for her statement first. She gave a lengthy, incoherent statement that she had written. Then, the judge asked for my statement. I said they had not paid rent in three months. He asked if I had given them legal notice to pay. I said yes. He then ruled in my favor that they had to leave the property in two weeks on a specific day. I had to take a written copy of that ruling to the sheriff's office so they could schedule a sheriff's officer to execute the order. I also had to go to the Sheriff's office and pay a fee for them to perform this duty (which seemed redundant since my taxes paid for the Sheriff's department). On the day of the eviction, the officer arrived in the morning and told my tenants they had to pack their belongings and vacate the property by 2 pm. The sheriff's officer had me meet him there at 2 pm to watch him physically demand them to leave. Then, I locked the property gate so they could not return.

The woman started out paying her rent with a pretty good job. Then it all went bad. I felt sorry for her, but I couldn't afford to pay the property costs without proper rent, and I could not fix her problem. The court also ruled that my former tenant owed me all the back pay plus some damage they did to the property, plus the expenses of the eviction. After they were evicted and gone, and I had another tenant, I went to the courthouse, and I forgave the debt of what she owed me. Ethically, I didn't have to. She owed me that money from the rental agreement. But I knew she was in trouble with drug addiction. I didn't want to add more to her problems with a court payment order. I could afford the loss more than she could. And it was worth it to me to not have to deal with it anymore.

I am saying all of this to show what property rights are. I bought it and had the right to use it for any legal purpose, including renting it. I had the right to evict someone who did not pay her rent. And I did. I also had the right to keep or forgive that previous tenant's court-ordered debt to me, but I forgave it. I also had the right to sell that property, which I eventually did. All because I had property rights.

7. Business Rights.

Business rights are an extension of property rights because they are something you can own. A business is a kind of property. It means people have the legal right to create, buy, or legally acquire a business, to use it for legal purposes, and to sell it as they wish. The government or others may not confiscate a business without an overwhelmingly just cause and fair compensation. And it may not be unjustly taxed or regulated out of business.

This is almost the same statement as property rights in the previous section. It is an important human right for the same reason. Like legal property ownership, legal business ownership in a good business environment is a key pathway out of poverty. Property and business rights are human rights because the freedom to rise out of poverty is a human right.

Poor communities are usually marked by the many difficult steps required to buy property legally. They are also usually marked by many difficult steps to legally start, own, and operate a business. So, what emerges are many small black-market businesses. The poor are entrepreneurial but trapped in policies that only allow them to operate small, inefficient businesses. They can't grow to become enterprises that scale wealth, innovate great things, employ many, lift an economy, and generate significant tax revenue for the community because they operate in the legal shadows. If they grow too big, advertise too much, employ too many, and set up operations in a major facility, the government will bust them for operating an illegal unregistered business.

De Soto explains it:

> *Because they are not incorporated, extralegal entrepreneurs cannot lure investors by selling their shares; they cannot secure low-interest formal credit because they do not have legal addresses. They cannot reduce risks by declaring limited liability or obtaining insurance coverage. The only 'insurance' available to them is that provided by their neighbors, and the protection that local bullies or mafias are willing to sell them. Moreover, because extralegal entrepreneurs live in constant fear of government detection and extortion from corrupt officials, they are forced to split and compartmentalize their production facilities between locations, thereby rarely achieving important economies of scale.*[40]

That's why Hernando De Soto's work with the Institute for Liberty and Democracy focuses on property and business rights as the two major foundations of solving poverty. After working in the poverty space, they concluded that the primary barrier to property and business rights is the efficient administration of them by the government, and the solution comes by changing the laws. The right policies solve it. As he puts it, "Law is the instrument that fixes and realizes capital."[41]

The characteristics of a nation or community with business rights look like this.

- It is easy and affordable to register a legal business.
- It is easy and affordable to provide business reports to the government.
- It is an easy and affordable cost for businesses to pay the business taxes.
- Government officials do not shake down business owners for bribes.
- Businesses are not burdened with unnecessary licenses.
- Businesses are not burdened with unnecessary regulations.

- There are business brokers that are easy to find, and it is an easy and affordable process to buy or sell a business, not including the cost of the business itself. The value of the business determines that.
- The laws, courts, and law enforcement officials protect businesses from theft, vandalism, or mafia-style shakedowns.

When these business rights prevail, a mass movement of businesses emerges from the shadows and becomes legal. They grow bigger and multiply wealth, making much more than the costs of their taxes and regulations. The government receives a huge tax revenue boost, giving it the resources to provide needed services.

Business rights are human rights that solve poverty and create human flourishing.

8. Low to Moderate Taxation.

Thou shall not steal (Exodus 20:15). Gary North, the author of *Christian Economics in One Lesson*, argues that government spending beyond the basic proper functions of government violates this commandment.

"There is no such thing as a free lunch." That's Milton Friedman's statement in the book he co-wrote with his wife, Rose Friedman, *Free to Choose*. His point was that everything of value has a cost, and someone always pays for it. If the government offers you something for free, understand that others had to pay for it with their taxes or depreciated money and inflated prices of goods. But someone always pays.

When the government takes your money to give it to others, that is not your choice. It is coercion, the opposite of freedom. Politicians never frame it in those terms. They always frame it in some ethereal sense that makes it feel like it's a free lunch paid for by no one.

"It's your money" was one of President Ronald Reagan's favorite statements. He urged people not to fall into the trap of thinking that what they earned automatically belonged to the government. It is yours, and you consent to what the government can have for the purposes you approve. That is why it is called Democracy and freedom.

The truth is that when the government takes money from you through taxes to give to others through benefits and programs, it takes part of your life. It takes your labor, energy, time, passion, and money to gain it. That taking of part of your life must be justifiable for the benefits you receive and approved by you. If it is not, it is theft. The more theft you face, the less you gain from your efforts to create income and wealth.

That's why low to moderate taxes promote economic growth for individuals and the economy. They result in less taking from people's lives, so they are willing to create more because they know they can keep and benefit from it.

Imagine running a convenience store and being plagued by thieves stealing your goods. Imagine if the biggest thief was a government agent who came in daily, armed to the teeth, in broad daylight, and calmly stole all he wanted, and you had no recourse. Your business would probably go broke. It's hard to make money when thieves are draining you dry. If that thief is the government, it's even harder because you must pay for it or close your business.

This is why economies always grow when taxes and regulations are cut. It reduces how much the government thug is taking from your store!

When you advocate for low to moderate taxation and regulation, you advocate for a better economy, less taking, and less organized government theft.

9. Low to Moderate Regulation.

According to Clyde Crews of the Competitive Enterprise Institute, the average American household's cost of government regulations on business in 2023 was $14,514, and the total cost to the economy was $1.939 trillion.[42] That was the largest single-budget item in American households, aside from housing.

The government regulates businesses to prevent harm to the public, to protect the environment, and to pick economic winners and losers according to whatever political agenda is in force. As is the case with government in general, the tendency in regulations is to make more of them. Government legislators and regulators live to legislate and regulate. They mark their success with their new laws and regulations. However, all regulations have a cost of liberty lost and a bigger hole in each citizen's economic bucket.

Some regulations are necessary to keep businesses legal, fair, and responsible. But clearly, it is an arena that can and has gotten way out of control with all the varying agendas. One major monster is the climate change agenda. Climate change activists see no limit to how much businesses should be regulated to address their dubious claims of dangerous man-made climate change. [43]

U.S. President Joe Biden enacted regulations limiting the drilling and production of oil and gas, making the U.S. dependent on foreign sources of oil and gas who produce it with much less environmental protection in the name of climate change. He also enacted regulations in the car industry that have every car manufacturing company scrambling to create money-losing electric vehicles, raising the costs of their conventional vehicles. The regulations and subsidies, meaning taxes taken from citizens to give to the EV (Electric Vehicle) manufacturers, suppressed the real cost of the average EV in 2023 by $50,000. Taxpayers pay this balance of the real cost.

Sound economics teaches us that if EVs are better economically and environmentally, the free market can and will discover that and buy them. Some pioneering entrepreneurs will take the risk of making and selling EVs at their real cost. The EVs will prove themselves worth it, more innovations will bring the costs down, and then EVs will replace conventional vehicles. However, as a matter of law and regulation, the issue is too jaded with political agendas to get a true answer about EVs' economic and environmental costs and benefits.

This is one case in point, but there are many cases where governments impose unnecessary costs on people and businesses that suppress living standards and economies. The rich are hurt the least, and the poor are hurt the most because they cannot afford it.

Low to moderate regulations grow economies and help the poor rise out of poverty by creating more jobs, providing easier pathways to work, and enabling the start and operation of businesses.

10. Anti-Corruption.

Several years ago, I and some colleagues attempted to drill a water well in a village in Western Kenya. We interviewed several Kenyan drilling companies and settled on one we liked and trusted. We went to the county offices in Kisumu to get a permit for the well. It took several trips, and the permit officer was bribed to receive it. We could have protested, but our local friends considered it a normal cost of business, which I understood.

We sent a major part of the payment for drilling the well to the driller. However, he disappeared and did not drill our well. One of our Kenyan colleagues pressed charges against the driller for fraud, but the case went nowhere. Later, some other friends and their ministry were able to get that well drilled with the help of Member of Parliament Jared Okelo, who represents Nyando County. They even got a county well drilling rig and crew on the job. They had the proper authority to bypass the regular corruption and get it done.

So, two people made some money. The agency permit guy made a little bit with the bribe. The well driller made a lot by stealing our money. However, I now work with a business investment firm that is interested in international opportunities. One current opportunity is in Kenya. I will be hesitant to recommend any investment in Kenya that does not protect us from bribes by officials, individuals who see any American money as an easy target for fraud, and courts that do not defend our rights as investors and business partners. That doesn't mean we wouldn't invest in any business in Kenya. This means that the bar must be higher than it is in many other places to protect us from the cost of corruption. And Kenya is much better on the corruption perception scale than many other countries.[44]

Corruption is worse in countries with high poverty, partly because their populations are less empowered to confront it and change it. Corruption benefits the few powerful players at the top of the system, but it suppresses outside investment by the private sector and the operation of successful businesses within the country. One study estimates that corruption costs the equivalent of a 20% tax on foreign investors.[45] For our water well project, the tax was 100%. No one does business under a 100% tax that results in a total loss.

That is what Ted Boers discovered in Haiti. He was a successful Christian businessman in the U.S. who spent seven years trying to build an agricultural business community there.[46] He continually faced the costs of corruption until finally, when their project had reached a critical point of success that required government approval, the government official in charge capriciously decided to deny it. Possibly because they had complained about corruption and bribes before. Boers was shocked that the government official in charge of the approval that would create tremendous benefit for Haitians would deny it out of spite or some other motivation than the good of the people. He, in essence, experienced a 100% tax on doing business in Haiti. He wrote *Demons of Poverty* about his experience. His thesis is that dark spiritual forces often drive the people in power in high-poverty spaces, and we better not be naïve about it if we are called to work there. It echoes the reality that every poverty space is surrounded by a class of elites who gain their power and money from the whole system that perpetuates poverty.

We discussed corruption under policy number two, The Rule of Law because it is a function of it. However, it is such a prevalent factor in the problem of poverty everywhere that it needs its own category. All countries need anti-corruption policies because of the tendencies of our fallen human natures.

Olga Irisova of the World Economic Journal summarizes it.

> *The elimination of corruption, according to the World Bank, in the long term can quadruple per-capita income and add 3% annual growth for all businesses. It turns out that a country with a per-capita income of, say, $2,000, that has started a campaign against corruption can expect per-capita income to increase to $8,000 over the long term. This is a good incentive to start taking action.*[47]

Corruption promotes poverty, and integrity promotes prosperity.

Any laws that violate these ten principles are bad laws.

Here is a list of these ten requisite policies that support the Spirit of Creation.

1. **Freedom: religious, political, and economic.**
2. **The Rule of Law.**
3. **Limited Government.**
4. **Marriage and Family.**
5. **Human Equality.**
6. **Property Rights.**

7. **Business Rights.**
8. **Low to Moderate Taxation.**
9. **Low to Moderate Regulation.**
10. **Anti-Corruption.**

Any laws that violate these policies are bad laws. Those that promote these policies, in moderation, can be good laws.

This leads us to the third condition in the Tree of Life that solves poverty and creates human flourishing: good infrastructure.

#3. THE BRANCHES ARE THE TEN INFRASTRUCTURES THAT SUPPORT THE SPIRIT OF CREATION

The next condition in solving poverty is good infrastructure. Often, poor or little infrastructure exists in high-poverty areas because the government funds are wasted on corruption or ineffective or inefficient programs.

My friend, Jared Okelo, whom we mentioned before as a Member of Parliament in Kenya for Nyando County, has led some desperately needed infrastructure projects in recent years in education, roads, bridges, and flood control of the Nyando River. These situations were so dire that one wonders what his predecessors were doing with their power and influence.

Here are the ten infrastructures that communities need to flourish. I will list them in a general order of priority and with little commentary, as they are self-evident. Sometimes, the order of priority changes because of local conditions.

1. **Safety:** from enemies, criminals, or government tyrants who threaten peace, life, health, possessions, property, or businesses.
2. **Water:** access to affordable, clean drinking water.
3. **Food:** access to grow and/or purchase affordable healthy food.
4. **Shelter and Clothing:** housing and clothing to protect from the elements.
5. **Utilities:** power, water, sewage treatment, and sanitation.
6. **Communications:** telephone and internet.
7. **Transportation:** roads, rail, and air to facilitate commerce and social life.

8. **Education:** K-12, vocational training, business training, and higher education.
9. **Health Services:** with freedom for private health care services.
10. **Financial Services:** for money payments, loans, investing, insurance, and the buying and selling of properties and businesses.

When we train community leaders on these ten infrastructures, we have them come to a consensus on the top three infrastructures they need but lack. Then, we have them prioritize that list with an aggressive plan to solve the first, then the next, and so on.

This leads us to the fourth condition required to solve poverty.

#4. THE FRUIT IS THE SPIRITUAL, SOCIAL, AND MATERIAL WEALTH CREATED BY THE PEOPLE

The fourth condition of the Tree of Life results from the first three conditions. When those conditions are met, the fourth condition happens. When people who are created in the image of God have a Spirit of Creation and the requisite policies and infrastructures that support the Spirit of Creation, they will create new value, own good properties, and grow good businesses. They will create prosperity and solve poverty.

When the good roots, trunk, and branches of the Tree of Life are in place in a culture, the people flourish.

It would be like planting a peach tree with good roots, trunk, and branches in good soil. Peaches will come naturally because it is the nature of the tree. The Tree of Life is a good metaphor for how to solve poverty because it reflects the nature of human nature and the nature of the world.

When people possess the spirit of poverty, live under bad policies, and lack infrastructure, they will naturally perpetuate poverty. The whole system is a bad tree planted in bad soil. It naturally produces little or no fruit.

We have shown how to fund our callings and solve poverty through the Spirit of Creation. Now, let's look at the third and final outcome promised by this book: how to Capitalize the Global Church.

Chapter Sixteen
Capitalize the Global Church

THE TREE OF LIFE IS a picture of how poverty is solved. When a Christian community has a culture of creating many Trees of Life, it becomes an Ecosystem of Creation. It has the Spirit of Creation, which *capitalizes* it with the knowledge, skills, and practices to fund its life and ministries.

The world needs Jesus for salvation, life change, and cultural change, but the ministries and works that produce these results must be funded. A capitalized Global Church is one where every Christian Community is an Ecosystem of Creation that creates many Trees of Life.

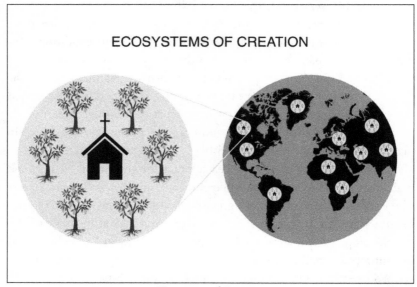

Ecosystem of Creation

The Church in the West inherited the Spirit of Creation from its forefathers. That heritage has produced Trees of Life and Ecosystems of Creation. However, that light of truth is disappearing, and the darkness of ignorance is growing under the pressures of secularist, socialist, and globalist philosophies, which are metastasizing in Western cultures. We must regain it to remain capitalized and fulfill our part of the Christian Mission.

For the Majority Church in the developing world, it's a different story. For the most part, it was not taught the Spirit of Creation by Western missionaries during the missionary phase of its development. They taught the gospel of salvation but not the Spirit of Creation. They delivered spiritual empowerment but not economic empowerment.

You can't travel among the Majority Church and not constantly see this elephant in the living room.

THE ELEPHANT IN THE LIVING ROOM

I was in a meeting not long ago in Dallas with the Bishop of a Christian denomination in Africa to discuss strategies for economic empowerment among their people. His immediate concern was that their historic mission hospital faced a financial crisis. It had been funded historically by charitable gifts from its sister denomination in the U.S. and several U.S. evangelical nonprofits. It also created revenue through its health services. However, they lacked funds to keep major parts of the growing hospital operating. They were also facing a crisis of diminishing and inadequate donations from the West. Its donor charities were having charity fatigue after many years of giving a lot of money. They seemed to think that the hospital should be self-supporting by now.

I drew the following diagram of how the global Christian movement goes in cycles of three phases. Phase I is the missionary phase. Phase II is transferring the Christian leadership from the missionaries to national leaders. Phase III is economic empowerment, where the national Christians learn how to fund their lives and ministries.

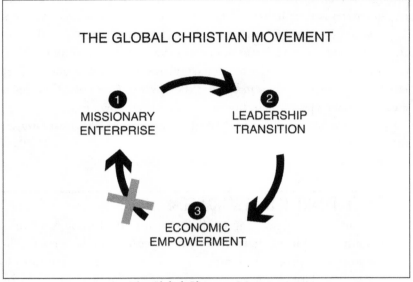

The Global Christian Movement

The large X on Phase III indicates where the world Christian mission with the Majority Church is stuck. He pointed his finger to the X and said, "This is where we are."

This crisis is a microcosm of the economics of the Majority Church in Africa, Asia, Latin America, and Oceania. They often have inadequate empowerment to fund their ministries and depend on support from the West. That means their part of the Christian Mission of making disciples and growing Christianity globally stops or slows down significantly with them. Endlessly funding them from the West is unsustainable because the source is limited. It is also counterproductive because it creates dependent passive serfdom and prevents proper biblical empowerment. This is the elephant in the living room of the Global Church. It is ubiquitous, and it suppresses the Christian Mission.

I began to talk to the bishop about creating ecosystems of creation in their denomination, hospitals, churches, communities, nation, and on their continent as the solution.

He told me of one attempt to make progress. "Our denomination has acquired quite a bit of property," he said, "so we called a meeting of our board to vote on a proposal to form a business to manage those properties for the economic benefit of our ministries. Seventy-eight African leaders of our denomination voted yes. Two American missionaries from our parent missions organization said, 'Not only do we vote no, but we want our no-vote to be video recorded.'"

This illustrates that this problem is partly rooted in bad theology and bad economics in the evangelical missions movement. It has not understood the Spirit of Creation and its role in funding the lives and ministries of the people it has served. It was not setting them up to succeed spiritually *and* economically, which are both necessary. It created a kind of Indian reservation-style socialist system of dependence.

Also, at our meeting with the Bishop, an American businessman said, "The top executive of that American missions organization called me. He said they own 100 acres of property in the county where they have their home office in the U.S., and he asked me to create a plan to generate some income from that property to benefit their organization."

There were six of us sitting at the table: four Americans and two Africans. We sat there in silence, taking in the irony. Actually, the hypocrisy.

American businesses fund that American missions organization. They give some of that money to the African denomination and its hospital. So, the African denomination and hospital are funded by business, but it's American business. So, why don't they promote the economic empowerment of businesses by the Africans in Africa to fund African ministries and works?

This is such a common problem it begs the question. *Why do some missions, nonprofits, and charities give free stuff but not empowerment?* At best, they don't know better. Or it may not fit their theological framework. At worst, as the documentary film *Poverty, Inc.* and the book *Toxic Charity* propose, some like the codependent relationship that keeps them in business and power. The first answer is the most common, but the last one is sometimes true.

A vision I suggested to the African bishop was this. Imagine:

- A movement to teach the Spirit of Creation throughout your denomination,

- A movement to teach it to your local communities through your churches,
- A movement to teach it to your whole country,
- A movement to create as many revenue streams from your hospital's health services as possible,
- A movement to create an ecosystem of businesses under a hospital development corporation for the benefit of the hospital,
- A movement to create Ecosystems of Creation in all churches, schools, ministries, and missions,
- The whole Christian community of your nation becoming an Ecosystem of Creation,
- Your whole country becoming an Ecosystem of Creation,
- Transporting that whole universe of creation to neighboring countries in Africa, and
- Creating and exporting human flourishing in all ways, globally, through the Church, in one generation.

Imagine that.

BY THE NUMBERS:

2.632 billion people claim to be Christians out of a total population of 8.1 billion.[48]

837 million Christians live in the Global North (Europe, Russia, and North America), or 32%.[49]

1.795 billion Christians live in the Global South and Majority World (Africa, Asia, Latin America, and Oceania), or 68%.[50]

Based on the statistics of poverty from multiple agencies, I would estimate the number of Christians who live in practical poverty in the Global South to be 1 billion.

These 1 billion Christians can't properly fund their lives and their churches, Christian schools, ministries, missionaries, properties, businesses, and community developments.

Imagine 1 billion Christians in the developing world becoming empowered over the next twenty-five years and the rest of the Global Church re-empowered to fund their life-changing and world-changing ministries.

We could flood the world with evangelism, discipleship, and cultural transformation from all directions to all places and people on earth.

We could unleash this sleeping giant within Christianity to change the world. But how can we do this? Here are four strategies.

FOUR STRATEGIES TO CAPITALIZE THE GLOBAL CHURCH

Capitalizing the Majority Church can be done through self-replicating Spirit of Creation movements. We can use the successful methodologies of the modern disciple-making movements by training national trainers, who train trainers, who train trainers. Of course, this is the biblical model of II Timothy 2:2, "Entrust the things you heard from me, in the presence of many witnesses, to faithful men who will also be able to teach others." (EHV)

Here are four disciple-making movement strategies that make sense for the Spirit of Creation movement.

First, equip national Christian leaders to create their self-sustaining empowerment movements.

Second, provide ongoing training support and encouragement. Movements die without ongoing nurturing.

Third, partner with national leaders through multiple generations, then leave it to them. Jesus left and entrusted the Christian mission to his disciples. The Apostle Paul started churches throughout the Roman Empire and left them to local leaders. A movement has not become sustainable and self-replicating until the local leaders own it and reproduce it. They can't own it and reproduce it fully until the missionaries leave.

Fourth, partner with them after leaving it to them. For a long time, the buzzword in Christian missions has been paternalism and how to avoid it. That means not treating the people we serve in missions like children but as adults and equals.

A key to moving from the paternalism inherent in a movement to fraternalism, where we treat each other as brothers and sisters, is to partner on projects where we call on each other's strengths and capabilities. We could do that on ministry, business, and community projects. Imagine partnerships of equals globally to partner in kingdom work. Imagine that being the normal practice in Christianity. It is already happening, but it needs to grow a lot more.

AN INDIAN ECOSYSTEM OF CREATION

Several years ago, while I was a pastor in New Mexico, I visited India with the missions leader Roscoe Brewer to help train church planters. Roscoe had been the leader of the missions department at Liberty University. He was famous for developing the SMITE Teams of college students who did missions work around the globe. He became focused on and influential in the unreached people group movement. He formed a ministry called EPIC International to reach unreached people groups in the 10-40 window[51]. The church planters we were training were part of that strategy.

That experience was a turning point for me. The economics of the experience was maddening, except for one Indian pastor who was inspiring.

Our team was training about seventy-five church planters from Northeast India, Nepal, and Bhutan in the Indian city of Siliguri. These church planters were surviving on fifty dollars a month from EPIC International. They would go to villages with virtually nothing but their witness and live very meagerly on one bowl of rice per day, which might have some vegetables and occasionally a little meat. It was the cheapest way to mobilize the most disciple-makers in the 10-40 window.

While we were at the training conference, we were told not to eat around the trainees because many were hungry and just lived that way. We fed them one big meal at midday: a massive plate of fried rice with vegetables and chicken. The catering group was made up of a caste of Indians who were short and thin people. These men worked shirtless over gas fires with giant woks, throwing in all the ingredients with a fantastic array of spices. The aroma was incredible. Watching those guys work, I felt like I was in a food and travel show. They saw my curiosity about all their open bags of spices and welcomed me to go to each one and smell and taste it.

Our trainees were also short and thin people, and I had never seen such little people eat so much food in one setting. But they were making up and stocking up as the poor often do when they can.

There was an evangelical Indian pastor of a strong church in Siliguri whom Roscoe wanted to recruit to partner with us in the training and the ongoing support of church planters in the region, but he was aloof.

Roscoe got him to agree to see us, so we visited him. We arrived at his church property on a major road on the edge of town. A large block fence surrounded it. Inside was a large block church, and across the dirt lot was a large chicken farm. The property was bustling with schoolchildren.

We went upstairs on the front end of the church to a large second-story apartment that was the pastor's home. Pastor Joseph and his wife greeted us there graciously and told us about their ministry. They had a large and growing church. They had a large Christian school that had a reputation in the community as the best private K-12 school. And they ran a chicken business. Some of their students supplemented their tuition by taking eggs from the chicken business and selling them on the streets of Siliguri after school.

This pastor had created an Ecosystem of Creation. He made an excellent church ministry and received some income from it. He created a great Christian school that met during the week in the church facilities, and he received some income from it. He bought a good piece of property on which he developed a church, home, school, and chicken business, and that property was growing in value. The chicken business also provided him with some income. I think he had several businesses. It looked like he also had an auto mechanic and metal fabrication business in the back of the property.

This pastor was different from most Indian Christian leaders we worked with. He was not subservient to us. He was independent and did what God had called him to do. He was not looking to impress us or to seek money from us. We had to go to him and try to recruit him to partner with us. He was economically empowered. His Ecosystem of Creation blessed his life, family, ministry, and everyone associated with it. He eventually agreed to attend our conference and partnered with our church planting ministry.

In contrast, during our mission in India, we heard presentations by young, talented Indians asking us for money to support their ministries almost daily. At first, it was interesting, but then it became frustrating. By the end of our tour, it was starting to anger me. I was not angry at the young Indian ministry leaders who were soliciting us to support their ministries, but at the Christian system that does not teach them the Spirit of Creation, but the spirit of solicitation.

It taught them that money for Indian Christian ministries is made in America, so they need to solicit Americans to fund their ministries. This spirit was in a vibrant country with economic growth and some brilliant and ingenious people.

It led me to envision what could happen if the spirit of charity were replaced with the Spirit of Creation in the new generation of Indian Christian leaders. What kinds of value could they create spiritually, socially, and economically? What properties could they buy and develop for their present works and future value? What types of businesses could they grow to fund every good thing in their lives? I believe the potential is massive, but it requires a massive change in worldview about the righteous work of creating economic value.

While we were in Siliguri, we took a day trip to Nepal. On the way, we stopped at a church not far from the Indian border. "That's one of the church buildings," Roscoe said, "built by a church-building ministry out of the U.S." We knew which one he was talking about. They had a big campaign to build thousands of churches in India for about $5,00 each. The problem was this church building was abandoned, overgrown with weeds, and the windows were broken. No Indian church had built it themselves or even wanted it. So, there it stood, a monument to well-intended but unproductive charity.

That trip to India started to solidify my thinking. There had to be a longer-term economic plan for those church planters who could not move from survival to living a decent life and supporting a family. They could live on survival means for a while, but it was not sustainable, regardless of how noble the task was. And the sending mission owed them a better answer.

Many Indian Christians, like all Christians, need to shift their worldview to create the resources they need for their lives and ministries.

And charity has its limits with diminishing returns. Giving people what they should and can do for themselves or what they don't want is counterproductive.

JOHN H. MORGAN

It was a key experience that moved me toward my conviction that we must capitalize the Global Church with the Spirit of Creation because the world needs Jesus. It takes both spiritual and economic empowerment to deliver his blessings. It takes whole people bringing God's whole truth to minister to whole persons throughout the whole world.

My vision is for every Christian community to create Ecosystems of Creation to fund their work of saving souls, solving poverty, and changing the world.

Our vision at People Prosper International is to empower a million people by 2030, 10 million by 2040, and 100 million by 2050.

For us and every Christian and organization concerned with the Christian Mission, this book raises questions about the appropriate uses of charity, responsibility, empowerment, and partnership. How can we know when and where to use each one?

Thankfully, the Bible answers these questions. We will look at them in the next chapter.

Chapter Seventeen
Charity, Responsibility, Empowerment, and Partnership

IF YOU HAVE STRONG FEELINGS of compassion for those in need, you may have chafed at this book with thoughts like, "Yes, but if we don't feed those poor children, they are going to get sick and die," and similar thoughts about many other situations where charity seems like the best answer.

My answer is there are appropriate situations for charity, responsibility, empowerment, and partnership. Understanding the differences between these times and situations can give us clarity in living righteously with our Christian brothers and sisters, our world in need, and our Christian mission. I see some important guidance on this in Galatians 6:1-10 and Jesus' parable of the Good Samaritan.

GALATIANS 6:1-10 AND THE PARABLE OF THE GOOD SAMARITAN

A guide for when each of these is appropriate is found in Galatians 6:1-10, and one partial application of it is found in Jesus' parable of the Good Samaritan. Let's begin with the text of Galatians 6:1-10. I am not satisfied with any English versions I have read for this passage because subtle nuances need to be seen to interpret it correctly. I believe all versions get it right in some places but miss it in others. So, we will use the NIV version as a basis and translate some words differently within their accepted possible meanings.

1 Brothers and sisters, if someone is caught in a sin, you who live by the Spirit should restore that person gently. But watch yourselves, or you also may be tempted. 2 Carry each other's burdens, and in this way, you will fulfill the law of Christ. 3 If anyone thinks they are something when they are not, they deceive themselves. 4 Each one should test his own actions. Then they can take pride in themselves alone, without comparing themselves to someone else, 5 for each one should carry his own load. 6 Nevertheless, the one who receives instruction in the word should share all good things with their instructor. 7 Do not be deceived: God cannot be mocked. A man reaps what he sows. 8 Whoever sows to please their flesh, from the flesh will reap destruction; whoever sows to please the Spirit will reap eternal life. 9 Let us not grow weary in doing good, for at the proper time we will reap a harvest if we do not give up. 10 Therefore, as we have opportunity, let us do good to all people, especially to those who belong to the family of believers.

As the Apostle Peter said about the Apostle Paul (II Peter 3:16), some parts of his epistles are hard to understand. This is one of those. It seems to jump around to different ideas but also has a common thread. I want to interpret this text in light of how we relate to other people economically. It applies to how we think about charity, responsibility, empowerment, and partnership.

CHARITY

This passage starts with,

1 Brothers and sisters, if someone is caught in a sin, you who live by the Spirit should restore that person gently. But watch yourselves, or you also may be tempted. 2 Carry each other's burdens, and in this way you will fulfill the law of Christ.

Let's note some keywords. First, this person is "caught" or "overtaken" in this situation, which is called sin. Next, the English word sin comes from the Greek *paraptoma*, which means to sidestep and can mean trespass. This person is "overtaken" in a "sidestep" or "trespass." It has become a burden, and they need help getting back on track. The word burden comes from the Greek *bare*. In this context, it means a weight that is too much to bear alone.

It could mean temptation overwhelmed them, and they got caught up in a sin. It could mean false teaching, like the legalism addressed in Galatians, got them sidetracked. It could mean the troubles of this life have overtaken them, and they have found themselves in financial trouble, which is a burden to them. They need help to get back on their feet. Paul's language in this passage switches between suggesting a sinful trespass and one's financial needs. Those following the Spirit avoid most of these things, although not all. And they should help restore their brothers and sisters in humility, lest they too fall.

The Good Samaritan demonstrated this in Jesus' parable in Luke 10:30-37. He restored the traveler who was beaten on the road and left for dead. The traveler might have been more careful about traveling where bandits prey on people, but he was overcome by them and left with the burden of being attacked and robbed, and he needed help.

And this is the principle of when charity is appropriate. It is applicable when the circumstances of life overcome people, and they need help to have enough to get back on their feet. Some are overwhelmed by the cultures of poverty in which they were raised. Some are overcome by the deaths or abandonment of their parents. Some are overcome by losses, crises, and disasters like disease, deaths, war, famine, natural disasters, corruption, and crime. It happens in the developed world and occurs in the developing world.

Charity is appropriate when life's troubles overcome people, and they cannot fix it on their own. That leaves a vast world of need that can be appropriately helped by charity. Most of us will have times when we need it, and we will see many times when we should give it.

Many Christian charities focus on these kinds of needs, and they are doing God's work. When we say that charity does not solve poverty, we don't mean to disparage these charities. They are solving immediate problems of need for the overwhelmed, which is righteous work, but they are not addressing the long-term need of solving poverty, which may not be their calling. That's okay. Some are called to do one or the other. Some are called to do both. Either is fine. My primary calling is to address the solution to poverty, so I strive to be clear about what does and what does not solve poverty. But God bless those called to serve the overwhelmed and over-burdened in this life in Jesus' name.

RESPONSIBILITY

Within this passage about helping people get back on their feet spiritually or physically, Paul drops some truth bombs about personal responsibility. Here they are.

> *4 Each one should test his own actions. Then they can take pride in themselves alone, without comparing themselves to someone else, 5 for each one should carry their own load. And…7 Do not be deceived: God cannot be mocked. A man reaps what he sows.*

In verse four, Paul changes from using the word from "burden" (*bare*) to "load" (*phortion*). A *phortion* is a proper personal responsibility that people should carry themselves. It is appropriate to help carry someone else's *bare* burden but not one's *phortion* load. An example of this was Paul's admonishment that "…if a man will not work, he shall not eat" in II Thessalonians 3:10. So, if a man can work but will not work, it is not proper to give him food that you worked for. You are not helping him. His hunger may be his last motivation to carry his own load and work.

This is the challenge of parenting. Our job is to transition our children from totally dependent babies for whom we do everything to independent, self-supporting, responsible adults who not only take care of themselves but can also help carry others' true burdens.

The theme of responsibility is emphasized with the truth that we reap what we sow. Much of what we get in life is a harvest of what we planted with our actions. When we plant good things with responsibility and follow the Spirit of God, we harvest good results. We harvest bad things when we are sinful, foolish, or not following the Spirit of God. This is the ultimate truth of personal responsibility. Much of what we get in life is a result of our choices.

The application is to not do for others what they can and should do for themselves. Sometimes, we give our children too much, and it stunts their maturation toward responsibility. Sometimes, we overdo it with charity and aid, and we stunt the recipient's personal growth toward responsibility and empowerment. When we do that, we treat them like children. The word for that is paternalism. Another word for it is enabling.

When we talk about funding our callings, solving poverty, and changing the world, we have to keep an eye out for honoring personal responsibility. We must own our responsibility and carry our workload, learning, growing, self-mastery, and managing our finances wisely. We must treat the poor with dignity by expecting them to do what they can and should to help themselves, as we are also helping them get on their feet. In the work of unleashing the Global Church, we should have them do all they can and should do to help themselves. Every need they have is not a call for us to give them more free stuff just because we can. Sometimes, it is an opportunity to teach them the Spirit of Creation so they can take pride in themselves and carry their own load.

I am working with a poor African church that is growing in its biblical economic empowerment. They have a project of roofing their church with sheets of tin. They have been making progress in creating more value and money individually and tithing to their church. So, they have been making progress on the roofing project. My organization helps them with some projects, but we are not helping them with this one. This one is within their capabilities. And when they complete it, they can "take pride in themselves" as it says in verse 4 of this passage. This is not sinful but noble pride in taking responsibility and carrying one's load.

Responsibility is appropriate when one's efforts should meet the need. When we short-circuit that relationship by stepping in and providing it, we act paternalistically toward the person and stunt their growth in responsibility and nobility. When we short-circuit God's system of reaping what one sows, we enable people to live with irresponsibility, pathologies, and addictions. God is much tougher on irresponsible people than most people are. His consequences can be very hard, but they are designed to change and grow the person to receive blessings in the future.

EMPOWERMENT

The idea of empowerment runs throughout this passage in the form of learning the truth of God and following the Spirit of God in doing it. Verse 1b says,

1 Brothers and sisters, if someone is caught in a sin, you who live by the Spirit should restore that person gently.

And verses 8 and 9:

8 Whoever sows to please their flesh, from the flesh will reap destruction; whoever sows to please the Spirit will reap eternal life. 9 Let us not grow weary in doing good, for at the proper time we will reap a harvest if we do not give up.

These verses say that those who become empowered to know the truth of God and to follow the Spirit of God, "you who live by the Spirit," are the ones who should restore those overtaken in a trespass. Then, it names the empowerment of following the Spirit of God and the destruction of following our flesh or our sin natures.

This empowerment comes from the truth of God and following the Spirit of God, whether it is the "spiritual" truths like what sins to avoid or "practical" truths like creating economic value. Empowerment is preventative and preparatory. It prevents many cases from being overcome spiritually or economically. And it prepares us to be more responsible and blessed.

This means we need to do the work of receiving and giving empowerment. As we have said, charity, although appropriate for some situations, does not solve poverty. What solves poverty is the Spirit of Creation.

The story of the Good Samaritan tells us he paid for the beaten traveler to recover from his injuries in an inn. The story is silent about what happened after the man recovered, but we can assume that the man could get back on his feet and responsibly carry his load once again. He may have even gained a new level of empowerment by learning he couldn't travel that road safely alone or without protection. There is no biblical indication that the Good Samaritan supported the man for the rest of his life after he had recovered. That would have been an insulting act of paternalism. It would be enabling. It could foster a spirit of victimhood and passivity.

Empowerment is almost always appropriate because it prevents us from being overcome by problems that we can't resolve and prepares us to carry responsibilities that bring greater blessings.

THE SPIRIT OF CREATION

PARTNERSHIP

Partnership happens when two or more people or groups of empowered people work together as roughly equals or in agreed-upon responsibilities to accomplish more than they could have accomplished on their own.

Paul speaks of an important partnership that was needing to be established in the Christian church when he speaks of providing good, including financial support, for those who were the teachers in the church. He says in verse 6, "Nevertheless, the one who receives instruction in the word should share all good things with their instructor."

In the middle of this context, which started out seeming like he was talking about helping to restore someone who had fallen in sin, he is now talking about supporting the pastors and teachers of the Christian church. This helps us understand that this is a bigger discussion about things like charity, responsibility, empowerment, and partnership.

This specific application is the truth that spiritual leaders should be financially supported by those whom they teach and lead because it is a partnership. The spiritual leaders work to provide spiritual support for their flocks. The people who receive that spiritual support work full-time in the marketplace, making a living. So, they are responsible for giving some of their earnings to the spiritual leaders in exchange for the spiritual care, value, and leadership they receive. It was the system of the Old Testament priesthood and temple, and it is the system of the New Testament church (I Corinthians 9:13-14). It is a partnership that accomplishes more together. It is the same relationship as a baker and a buyer of bread. It is a fair and responsible exchange of value with one another. The relationship keeps the baker alive with a living and the buyer alive with his bread. The pastor nourishes his people's spirits, and the people keep him alive with support for his living. It is a fair partnership.

The immediate point is we should support our pastors, teachers, and spiritual leaders so they can do their work that benefits us and many others. The broader principle is that partnerships are often the best way we relate to each other to accomplish the best things. There have been some great partnerships where people accomplished greater things together. These partnerships combine and enhance the genius of the different gifts God gives people in the world, specifically the church.

John H. Morgan

In the work of the Global Church, one of the lagging opportunities that has been delayed because of an over-reliance on charity and an under-utilization of empowerment is the power of partnerships. As Christians worldwide become empowered spiritually and economically, more opportunities arise for great partnerships.

My nonprofit, PPI, and I are in the middle of a partnership with George Kienga in Kenya. (We told his story in Chapter One.) We taught him the Spirit of Creation in 2010. Since then, he has created an Ecosystem of Creation in his rural area outside of Awendo in Migori County, Kenya. His developments have included Golden State Academy, training programs for adults in the Spirit of Creation, Kienga Farms and Harvesting, Emmanual Medical Clinic, and his Annual PPI Youth Conference. The amazing thing is that George and his Kenyan partners have funded all of it, except for a couple of very small projects for which we gave a couple of thousand dollars.

George asked me for help acquiring a hematology analyzer and a microscope for his medical clinic. They cost $5,000 and are out of reach for them, but they can make a big difference in the effectiveness of their clinic in providing healthcare. Seeing George's empowerment, I offered him the option of a loan for the $5,000 that would be repaid from the clinic's income. I offered a partnership. That was not cruel that I didn't just give him the money. That was respect for his capability and empowerment.

He gladly jumped at the opportunity. We provided him with a loan with fair interest that was lower than he could get in Kenya. He repays it in monthly installments for three years. It meets his need without paternalism, with the responsibility to carry his load, with honor for his empowerment, and with the dignity of a partnership where we both have skin in the game. It gives him the pride of doing it himself. He is diligent about it and takes pride in each payment he makes. The small interest we earn helps us fund other projects.

He has future projects in mind that would require bigger loans. This is a step of growth for him to demonstrate faithfulness over a few things to become trusted with greater things. It's how the world of business partnerships through loans works.

"You have changed my life," George often writes in his What's App messaging, "and I thank God for you." My relationship with George has

184

been one where we have tried to act appropriately with charity, responsibility, empowerment, and partnership.

One of the principles of good partnerships is that each partner needs to have the right amount of skin in the game. Often, when we deal with the poor, we don't ask them for any skin in the game. We are just in giveaway mode and can't see the bigger picture. But this is insulting because it does not recognize that they have God-given dignity, intelligence, and gifts.

For years, when we have gone into poverty spaces to teach Christian communities about the Spirit of Creation, the mode that the missionaries or even the national Christians have been that we pay for...

- Our costs to get there,
- Their travel to get there,
- Their lodging at the event,
- Their food at the event,
- Their notes, paper, and pens for the event, and
- Their travel home.

Their skin in the game was their time and energy to take a paid trip and to pay attention to the training.

After a while, we realized something was wrong. We were not asking them for any skin in the game. So now we ask them to invest what they can and should at their level of economic empowerment. They pay for their children to go to school because they value it. If they value becoming personally empowered to rise out of poverty, they should pay some of what they can afford, even if it is just pennies or bringing an egg or a packed lunch.

We have done training events where we paid for everything, and people came in large numbers, mostly, I think, for the hot lunch of chicken and rice served at noon. However, very few of them took the training seriously and applied it. What they got for free was not valued. It's human nature the world over.

Skin in the game is relative. It may cost us more in dollars than what they pay in their currency, but it took less effort for us to get those dollars than it takes them to get an equivalent amount of dollars. I am not saying they must have equal dollars invested in any partnership. They should make a fair amount of effort for the value they gain. One of the principles of economics from Adam Smith is that the price of everything is equal to the effort it takes to gain it.[52] That's a good principle for understanding a fair partnership.

It can cost us $7,000 to present multiple training conferences for several weeks across East Africa, but we are not asking our national attendees or host churches to pay for our expenses or to match our costs. We are asking them to pay their share with fair effort. We ask attendees to pay for their bus fare to the event, for church members to host attendees in their homes, for everyone to pitch in for the food or to bring their lunch, and for everyone who can bring a pen and a notepad. We are increasingly asking people to pay at least a small price for training.

I just spoke with the leaders of a major U.S. seminary who returned from a multi-week trip to an African country. While there, they paid for everything listed above and a stipend for each of the 500 who attended a two-day conference. They were shocked at the amount they were paying others to attend. It left them wondering if the attendees had enough skin in the game.

Partnerships are agreements between individuals or groups of individuals to commit fair amounts of effort to a common cause in exchange for the benefits they receive. The results can be greater than what could have been accomplished without the partnership.

As I look at the trajectory of the Global Church, I believe we will see a surge of global partnerships that will create massive amounts of spiritual, social, and economic value.

GUIDELINES FOR CHARITY, RESPONSIBILITY, EMPOWERMENT, AND PARTNERSHIP

This text by the Apostle Paul wraps up with this admonition in verse 10 of Galatians 6, "Therefore, as we have opportunity, let us do good to all people, especially to those who belong to the family of believers." Doing good can be our best when we follow the principles of charity, responsibility, empowerment, and partnership.

When we see human needs, we can follow these six questions as guidelines for using charity, responsibility, empowerment, or partnerships.

1. Is/are this person or these people overwhelmed by the troubles of life that they need help to resolve? If so, charity may be the best response.
2. Is this person suffering bad consequences from not being responsible for a load they could and should carry? If so, gentle correction and encouragement may be appropriate.
3. Does this person need more empowerment to carry more responsibility and receive more blessings in the future?
4. Are my actions with people leading them toward sustainable responsibility and blessings?
5. Would a partnership be the best way for both parties to create the best outcome?
6. What is a fair amount of effort or investment for each party in this partnership to create the best outcomes?

These questions are guidelines. The final arbiters are the Holy Spirit's leading, your conscience, and your wisdom. You obviously can't give to every legitimate charity situation, or you would go broke. But you can give to the people whom the Spirit leads you. The same goes for all relationships of responsibility, empowerment, and partnership.

Charity is appropriate when life's troubles overtake people, and they need help getting back on their feet. *Responsibility* to carry one's load is always appropriate. *Empowerment* (spiritually and economically) puts people in a position of blessing and strength to resource their lives and to help others. We should be doing much more of it.

Partnerships of empowered people can create some of the greatest results. Those partnerships should be characterized by everyone having the right amount of skin in the game. I believe some of the greatest partnerships in the Global Church to change the world are just ahead.

Let's use these principles to "do good to all people, especially to those who belong to the family of believers."

This completes the application of The Spirit of Creation to Fund Your Calling, Solve Poverty, and Capitalize the Global Church with guidance on using Charity, Responsibility, Empowerment, and Partnership.

The last chapter wraps up the whole book with a story and a blessing.

Chapter 18
Go Forth and Conquer!

MY FRIEND CODY IS LIVING out the Spirit of Creation.

He pastors an excellent church in New Mexico. He leads a nonprofit initiative that provides mentors in the public schools in his community to help students emotionally, socially, and academically. He is a leader in foster parenting and helps fund an orphanage in Kenya. He is also a business entrepreneur with multiple business units of an entertainment franchise in multiple cities and states.

He wants to scale his business to fund his ministries and nonprofit works. He also wants to have a transformational impact on the lives of his employees, mostly young people. He wants to impact them spiritually, socially, and economically with God's best purposes for their lives.

He is living his calling, solving poverty, and changing the world. Imagine a world filled with Codys in every sector of work and culture.

You don't have to be a pastor, a nonprofit leader, and a business entrepreneur to live out the Spirit of Creation. That's not my point. You must live out your true calling from God, and the Spirit of Creation is God's plan to fund it.

There are thousands of ways to do it. You can do it as a rancher, farmer, athlete, artist, engineer, scientist, minister, politician, government worker, teacher, professor, businessperson, lawyer, doctor, accountant, writer, or craftsman. And that barely scratches the surface of the possibilities in God's creative purposes for his people.

THE SPIRIT OF CREATION

The Spirit of Creation is a biblical worldview of human flourishing. Technically, it is a theological economy of human flourishing. It teaches God's way for people to be blessed spiritually, socially, and economically. It is the source of the best and most sustainable wealth for individuals and nations.

The Spirit of Creation is not only a worldview but a person. He is the divine person of God's Holy Spirit. He is the Spirit of Creation. He created all things, and He filled man with the breath of life; He created man in his image; He blessed human beings and gave them the commission to create new value to make their livings, help others, bless the world, and worship God. And He leads his people individually by His Word, providence, and presence within them to "will and to act according to His good purpose" (Philippians 2:13). He is the author of the truths of the biblical worldview that is the Spirit of Creation.

So, in this last chapter, let me call you to follow the biblical worldview of the Spirit of Creation and its author. Let me call you to follow the Holy Spirit.

SEVEN ACTIONS

Let me challenge you to do these seven actions to live out your calling from the Spirit of Creation.

1. Answer the WHAT, WHY, and HOW questions about your calling and follow the Spirit of Creation in living it out in your CREATE, OWN, and GROW economic actions.
2. Create the best value you can. It will provide the income you need.
3. Own the best property you can. It will help you grow the wealth you need.
4. Grow the best business you can. It will help grow the income and wealth you need. You can do that as an entrepreneur, an intrapreneur, or an investor. Or any combination of these three.
5. Get involved in a good church.
6. Partner with a group, like People Prosper International, Global Advance, or Buckner International, that does an excellent job of empowering the Global Church with the Spirit of Creation.
7. Lead a small group through a study of this book. It will empower you to fund your calling, solve poverty, and capitalize on the Global Church. The group can be young people, men, women, couples, retirees, or those in a prison ministry.

REDEEMING YOUR TIME

I have lived with a sense of urgency about the shortness of life and the need to live my life on my calling as best as possible. When I was a senior in high school, I brought the bachelorette message to my senior class at my public high school on the topic of the brevity of life from James 4:14, "You do not know what will happen tomorrow. For what is your life? It is even a vapor that appears for a little time and then vanishes away."

You can imagine how much more I believe it now. At my age, I have seen the deaths of many friends, colleagues, church members, and family members. A shocking number of them died before they reached my current age.

There are four things that I believe now more than ever.

- My time is limited.
- My talent is limited.
- My energy is limited.
- My mental space is limited.

Therefore, I don't have the time, talent, energy, or mental space to waste on things that are not right in the middle of my calling. I'm not saying I don't have time for family, friends, fun, rest, and recreation. I have those things in balance with my work for a full and healthy life. I don't have time for things that waste my time, talent, energy, or mental space on things outside of my calling, my most important relationships, and times of restoration.

Frequently, I experience new things that remind me that we have these limitations.

FAREWELL, SHEM

Recently, on his fiftieth birthday, my dear friend in Nairobi, Kenya, Shem Okello, felt very tired and short of breath. Then he started feeling chest pains. They rushed him to the hospital and tried to stabilize him, but they could not save him. He died of a heart attack.

I and many others were shocked because Shem epitomized calling, vision, leadership, ministry, business, action, and energy to interact with people. He was the anchor many people counted on to give stability and hope.

Shem graciously helped us start teaching the Spirit of Creation principles to key people in Kenya. He sat in on that early teaching, and it revolutionized his life. He became a multi-ministry leader, a multi-property owner, and a multi-business entrepreneur. He taught those principles in Kenya, Uganda, and Tanzania. The pinnacle of his spiritual, social, and business leadership was his co-founding the for-profit Emmanuel Community Hospital with his friend, Dr. Shem Okumu, in the Chakaa neighborhood of Nairobi.

Shem was our anchor for our work in Africa until God took him home. I thank God He had Shem there to partner with us when He did. Now, God is raising up more leaders in multiple countries.

I loved many things about Shem, but my favorite was his sense of humor. He was always seeing the humor in things and making people laugh. He was a fantastic co-teacher with me of these principles in Africa. I would teach the principles, and then he would get up and tell stories about practicing them, moving back and forth from English to Swahili or Luo, and he would have the crowd rolling in the aisles. I could understand the gist of it, and he had me rolling in the aisles.

Shem was the example of what we are challenging African Christians and all Christians to become. He was a spiritually and economically empowered person. He was empowered with the Spirit of Creation. If all Christians globally lived like Shem, the Church would turn the whole world upside down with the kingdom of God. Souls would be saved, poverty would be solved, and the kingdom of God would come in amazing ways.

I look forward to seeing Shem again in heaven and having a big laugh. It will be good to talk about what God did in our lives and through us in our times on earth. We may say something like, "That sure was fun but short, and we have this perfect eternal home now. No more striving to grow Christ's kingdom against opposing forces. We are in his perfect eternal kingdom now, so what should we create next?"

Until then, farewell, Shem. Thank you for your partnership, and I will see you soon in glory, Brother.

GO FORTH AND CONQUER!

My wife and I have five children. Three daughters and two sons. When they were growing up and leaving our house to go to something good, like school, youth group, work, or to hang out with their friends, we would say to them, "Go forth and conquer!"

We were saying, *"We bless you* because God created you in his image. So be fruitful, multiply, fill the earth, subdue it, and take dominion of it. Go out in the world and use your gifts, talents, and passion to create new value."

That has become a standard blessing I give at the end of training sessions on the Spirit of Creation.

So, let me speak this blessing over you...

God has created you in his image, saved you by his grace through Jesus Christ, and indwells you by His Holy Spirit. Therefore, be fruitful, multiply, fill the earth, subdue it, and take dominion of it. Create value, own property, and grow business...and as you are going, make disciples of everyone you can and everywhere you can. In short...

Go Forth and Conquer!

Notes

1   https://www.ourworldindata.org/malaria/introduction. Accessed 6.14.23.

2   Charles Colson and Nancy Pearcey, *How Now Shall We Live?*,
    (Wheaton, Illinois: Tyndale House Publishers, 1999) 295-296.

3   Martin Luther King, Jr., *Letter from Birmingham
    Jail* (csuchico.edu). Accessed 6.14.23.

4   Tim Hargrove, *My Limiting Beliefs*. (www.
    peopleprosper.org/resources), 2023.

5   St. Augustine, Confessions, trans. John K. Ryan (New York:
    Doubleday and Co. Inc., 1960), bk. 11, chs. 13 & 30.

6   Note: Hebrews 2:16.

7   A word study using www.biblehub.
    com>interlinear>genesis>1>28. Accessed 04.26.23.

8   Ephesians 2:1-10.

9   Romans 1:18-32.

10 Genesis 4:19-22.

11 Michael A. Eisenberg, *The Tree of life and Prosperity: 21st Century Business
    Principles from the Book of Genesis* (New York: Wicked Son, 2021), 53-61.

12 Adam Smith, And Inquiry into the Nature and Causes of the Wealth of
    Nations, Michael Lewis, Ed., *The Real Price of Everything: Rediscovering
    the Six Classics of Economics* (New York: Sterling, 2007), 22.

13 Javier Milei's first speech as president of Argentina. Buenos Aires
    Times. December 10, 2023. Accessed 10.30.24 www.batimes.com.ar.

14 Henry Hazlitt, *Economics in One Lesson*, (New
    York: Three Rivers Press, 1946), 139.

15 George Gilder, *Wealth and* Poverty, (Washington DC: Regnery Publishing, Inc., 2012), 102.

16 https://www.goodreads.com/quotes... Accessed 7.7.23.

17 https://www.mckinsey.con/industry-financial-services/the-rise-and-rise-of-the-global-balance-sheet... Accessed 7.7.23.

18 Hernando De Soto. The Mystery of Capital: Why capitalism triumphs in the West and fails everywhere else, (New York: Basic Books, 2000), 39-67.

19 A word study using www.biblehub.com>interlinear>genesis>1>28. Accessed 04.26.23.

20 https://www.benvaugh.com/uncovering-john-lennons-real-estate-portfolio. Accessed 7.10.23.

21 Max Weber, *The Protestant Ethic and the Spirit of Capitalism*, trans. Stephen Kalberg (Los Angeles, CA: Roxbury Publishing Co., 2002) xxix-xxx.

22 The editors, How Bernie Sanders Became a Millionaire. https://www.townandcountrymag.com/society/politics/a31437248/bernie-sanders-net-worth/

23 https://en.wikipidia.org/wiki/You'll...own...nothing... . Accessed 9.1.2023.

24 Twitter @Chief Nerd 8/25/23 quoting Robert F. Kennedy, Jr. about Blackrock's plan to buy every private residence. Citing Richmond.com/news/state-reg... *Robert F. Kennedy Jr. brings economic message to campaign stop.* Aug. 23, 2023. Accessed 9.1.2023.

25 Jeff Haden, Inc Magazine, *64 Years Ago Ray Kroc Made a Decision That Completely Transformed McDonald's.* Nov. 16, 2020. https://www.inc.com/jeff-haden/64-years-ago-ray-kroc... Accessed 9.5.23

26 Michal Eisenberg, *Tree of Life*, 53-66.

27 www.invent.org/John-Deer. Accessed 8.26.2024.

28   Gene L. Green. *The Letters to The Thessalonians*. The
      Pillar New Testament Commentary. (Grand Rapids,
      MI: Eeerdmans Publishing, 2002), 341-356.

29   Max Weber, Ibid.

30   Charles Dickens, *A Christmas Carol*, (London:
      Chapman and Hall, 1843), 3.

31   Xavier Egan, *Silver Tsunami: Navigating the Wave of Small Business
      Succession*. www.minoritybusinessreview.com. Accessed 11.4.24.

32   James Royal and Arielle O'Shea, *What is the Average Stock Market
      Return?*, NerdWallet.com. Accessed May 2024 at https://www.
      nerdwallet.com/article/investing/average-stock-market-return.

33   Tony Robbins, *The Holy Grail of Investing*, (New
      York: Simon & Schuster, 2024), 5.

34   S Pearce Carey, *William Carey*, (London: Wakeman Trust, 1993).

35   Michael Matheson Miller, "The Prosperity Pyramid Scheme,"
      Religion & Liberty (Fall 2023): berty (Fall 2023): 28-39.

36   Miller, "The Prosperity Pyramid Scheme," 38-39.

37   Miller, Ibid, 36.

38   Miller, Ibid. 39.

39   Margaret Mead, Quote. Accessed April 2024, https://
      www.brainyquote.com/margaret_mead_100502.

40   De Soto, *Mystery of Capital*, 155.

41   De Soto, Ibid, 157.

42   Clyde Waybe Crews, *Here's How Much Regulations Cost the
      Average American Family – And How Biden is Making it Worse*,
      The Daily Signal. November 29, 2023. Accessed April 17,2024
      at https://cei.org/citationss/exclusive-heres-how-much...

43   Brent Bennett and Jason Isaac, Overcharged Expectations: Unmasking the True Costs of Electric Vehicles, Texas Public Policy Foundation, October 2023. Accessed April 17, 2023 at http://www.texaspolicy.com.

44   Olga Irisova, *The Cost of Corruption*, World Economic Journal, August 2014. Accessed April 17,2024 at htpps:// www.worldeconomicjournal.co/the-cost-of-corruption.

45   Olga Irisova, *The Cost of Corruption*.

46   Ted Boers, *Demons of Poverty: one entrepreneur's experience with addressing poverty in Haiti,* (Grand Rapids, MI: Acton Institute, 2017)

47   Olga Isirova, *The Cost of Corruption*.

48   *Status of Global Christianity, 2024, in the Context of 1900-2050.* The Center for the Study of Global Christianity at Gordon-Conwell Theological Seminary. Accessed Apil 2024, https://www.gordonconwell.edu/wp-content/uploads/ sites/13/2024/01/Status-of-Global-Christianity-2024.pdf.

49   *Status of Global Christianity, 2024.*

50   *Status of Global Christianity, 2024.*

51   The 10-40 Window is between the 10th and 40th parallels on the global map and where it intersects Africa and Asia exist the most people groups that are unreached by Christianity.

52   Adam Smith, *Wealth of Nations.* Quote accessed April 2024, https://www.forbes.com/quotes/106/.

For More Resources Please Visit
The People Prosper
International Website

www.peopleprosper.org/resources

Some of our resources:

- Study Workbook.
- Video Lessons.
- Small Group lessons.
- K-12 Curriculum.
- College and Seminary Courses.
- Speakers.

Inspire Your Child To Be a Value Creator
with Mia's Dream

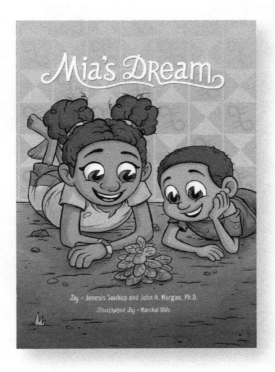

Mia's Dream

A beautifully written and color-illustrated story about a girl and her friend who learned how to create resources as part of her God-given purpose.

Available at Amazon.com and other booksellers